HOW TO SPEAK LIFE
SHARING YOUR FAITH IN 321

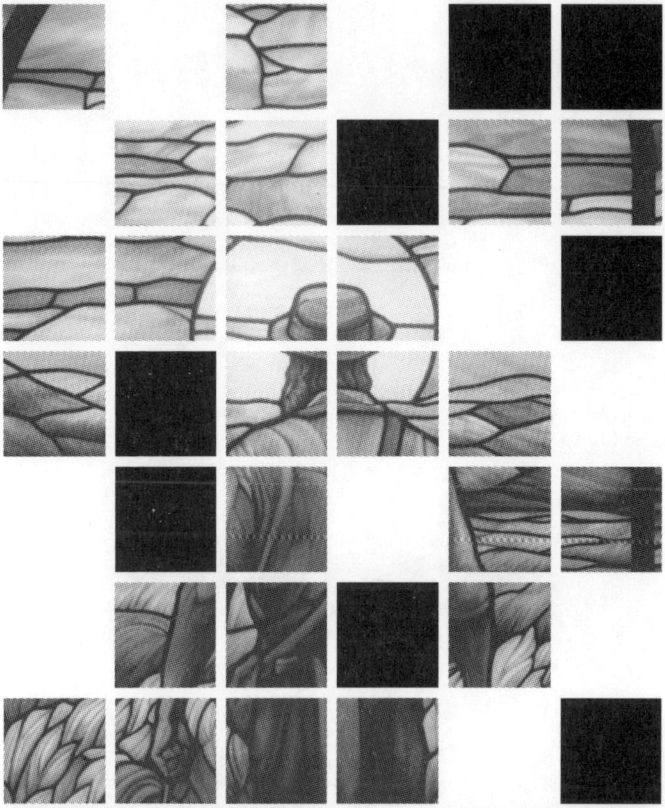

HOW TO SPEAK LIFE SHARING YOUR FAITH IN 321

Glen Scrivener

10 Publishing
a division of 10ofthose.com

British Library Cataloguing in Publication Data

A record for this book is available from the British Library

ISBN: 9781915705075

Cover design by Sparks Studio

Internal typeset by Pete Barnsley (CreativeHoot.com)

Printed in Denmark

10Publishing, a division of 10ofthose.com

Unit C, Tomlinson Road, Leyland, PR25 2DY, England

Email: info@10ofthose.com

Website: www.10ofthose.com

1 3 5 7 10 8 6 4 2

TO EMMA,
THE REAL EVANGELIST
OF THE FAMILY.

CONTENTS

321

INTRODUCTION

THE MISSION FIELD

I want people to know Jesus—my family, my friends, my neighbours, everyone. But it's tricky. When it comes to faith, the people in my life are in so many different places.

Some of them think Christianity is the worst. They reckon it's bigoted, controlling, anti-science, regressive—just awful. In their hearts they manage (I think—I *hope!*) to absolve me personally, but they figure I've been swept up in something Very Bad. These friends are a minority though.

Far more of my friends and neighbours shrug their shoulders and say, 'Good for you, Glen, whatever gets you through the night.' Perhaps they've even had some experience of faith in the past. But if they have, they feel it's no longer for them. Still, they're far from hostile.

Then there are those with more of a Christian history. It could be distant, it could be recent, it could be positive, it could be poisonous. For these friends it's complicated. There is a genuine attraction to Christ (or there used to be), but there are also a thousand distractions and obstacles in their way.

And then there are the total surprises. Some friends shock me by being open to the gospel all of a sudden. Like a month ago when a friend—*out of nowhere*—confided in me: 'I realised over the summer I don't know anything about the Bible.' He's since taken himself and his family off to church every Sunday.

Think of your own family, friends, neighbours and work colleagues. Do you recognise these kinds of categories? I didn't pick them at random. These four types of people map onto the four types of soil Jesus spoke of in Matthew 13. Remember the parable: God's kingdom grows like seed. But the seed, representing God's Word, gets scattered across all kinds of ground: the path; the rocks; the thorns; and the good soil.

Jesus goes on to explain what these 'soil types' refer to. First there's the path where birds come and gobble up the seed. This represents flat out resistance—even satanic opposition—to the gospel. The Word is meant to take root in our *hearts* but instead we find hearts that are 'calloused' (v15) and resist the message of the kingdom.

Next there's stony soil. This represents a shallow reception of the Word that soon shrinks back from real commitment. After that come a tangle of thorn bushes. These represent 'the worries of this life and the deceitfulness of wealth' (v22), choking whatever faith may lie beneath. Finally comes the good soil which receives the Word deeply and enduringly.

This is the mission field. Responses are mixed, to say the least. And if we're the ones holding out the Word of life to friends and family, how will it look? 'Hit and miss'—and mainly miss.

I'm guessing that's how your evangelism feels. Mine certainly does. 'Evangelist' is my day job and yet, when

I report to my board of trustees every quarter this could be the headline every single time: *Hit and miss—mainly miss.*

THE POWER OF THE SEED

Imagine a Martian came down to see the farmer in the parable at work. He'd be puzzled. What good can it do to scatter such tiny particles on the ground? What *are* those little granules he's littering all over the place? It looks like a hopeless activity. Even if you explained to the Martian about seeds and germination, the sower seems to be the least strategic farmer in the history of agriculture. *Who sows on the path? Surely not among rocks? And, mate, the thorns? Seriously?*

I know nothing about farming but even I think to myself: What about a scarecrow? Maybe dig the rocks out? If there are thorns, surely you should spray them, or cut them back, or weed them out…? Please do something—*anything*—instead of throwing fistfuls of precious seed at frankly hopeless situations.

But no. There is no plan B for this farmer. Or C, or D. It's all plan A, and a very rudimentary plan it is: sow the seed. The power is not in the farmer's delivery, cutting-edge technology or brilliant new strategy. The power is entirely in the seed. And isn't that encouraging?

Earlier I said the seed is God's Word, and it is (Mark 4:14). But let's think more deeply about God's Word because, ultimately, *Jesus* is the Word of God—the eternal Word (John 1:1–2). And a very early title for Christ in Scripture appears in Genesis 3:15, which promises the coming Seed of the woman (or 'Offspring', it's the same word in Hebrew). It was prophesied right from the beginning that this Seed would be born of a woman to crush Satan, though he himself would be struck. The oldest, most enduring gospel promise of the Scriptures was the promise of 'the Seed'.

When Jesus came—when the Word became flesh—he likened himself to a seed that must be buried (John 12:24). But what happens to seeds when they are buried? That isn't the end. It's only the beginning.

And so, through Christ—the Seed—being crucified and buried, he would rise again to give new life. Such is the nature of seeds: *down they go* into the darkness of the earth, then *up they rise* to bring life and nourishment to the world. Jesus promises exactly that. He would be the first to die and rise, but he would pioneer a way of life for all his followers (John 12:24–26).

Once a seed 'dies' and rises again it becomes a tree which contains fruit and the fruit contains many more seeds—seeds 'according to their kind'. Jesus has risen from the dead to give us his kind of life and his kind of seed. Now *we* have the Word of life and we can scatter that same seed. This is the life we've been swept up into. The Word gave us life and now we have become those who speak life to others.

This book is about sharing your faith. In a deep sense it's about scattering seeds. But the power is not in your method of sowing. You don't have to do in-depth cultural analysis of your friend's particular 'soil type'. You don't have to learn the secret of effective delivery. You don't have to prepare Plans B, C and D as a back-up. It's not about you and your skills, it's all about the seed and its power.

So out we go into the world to sow the word of Jesus. What should we expect? From one point of view it will be hit and miss—there'll be birds and thorns and rocks. But Jesus gives us another perspective in Matthew 13.

WORLD DOMINATION

A single apple pip can feed the world. Imagine it: if the seed goes into the ground and rises again, it produces a tree. From that tree will come dozens of apples and hundreds of seeds. Plant those seeds and you'll get thousands in the next generation. By the sixth generation you'll have enough apples to feed the world.

Seeds are easily overlooked yet have tremendous power—just like the Word:

> *He told them another parable: 'The kingdom of heaven is like a mustard seed, which a man took and planted in his field. Though it is the smallest of all seeds, yet when it grows, it is the largest of garden plants and becomes*

a tree, so that the birds come and perch in its branches.'
MATTHEW 13:31–32

Here in Matthew 13, Jesus rounds off his seed parables with the simplest yet most striking of them. He is in no doubt where his kingdom is headed. Though it looks weak and despised, one day his kingdom will conquer the world.

It takes time. Farming is not about instant results, but in the end the seed is victorious. It gets to the point where the birds perch in the tree grown by the word of Jesus. At the start of Matthew 13 the birds seemed so much greater than the seed. They devoured it, seeming to snatch away all hope in satanic opposition. And yet, if you just let the seed do what the seed does, even the greatest enemies of the kingdom are dominated by, and dependent upon, Christ's kingdom.

Even those who think Christianity is 'the worst'—bigoted, cruel, restrictive and regressive—do so by perching on the kingdom values of Jesus. He has taught the world what is 'best'. He has taught us *all* to value equality, compassion, freedom and progress. For more on *how* the word of Jesus grew such a kingdom you can read my book *The Air We Breathe*.

But if you want to be part of the ongoing advance of this kingdom—if you want to learn to speak life in our own generation—read on. It's all about a day-by-day work: unsung, untidy, undaunted, unhurried. It's about scattering the word of Jesus near and far, all the while knowing nothing, ultimately, can stop this seed growing. The word of Jesus will conquer the world.

COMING UP:

EIGHT SEEDS TO SCATTER

Sowing the word is for everyone. Yes, there are capital-E evangelists—those specifically gifted by the Spirit and called by the church. But this book is to help you speak life whatever your gifting or role. In each chapter I give an example of a one-on-one conversation I've had. All of them were unplanned. But in the middle of ordinary life sometimes opportunities arise. And I want us to be ready. How? By filling our pockets with seed.

Alongside these example conversations, I'll be giving you a different seed in each chapter. By the end of the book you'll have eight sentences or questions which you can sow into your conversations.

These are not clever strategies or polished presentations. I don't want you to be an advertising executive. I want us all to be profligate farmers, chucking seed like it's confetti. Unimpressive. Messy. But, by the Spirit, somehow life springs up. The power is not in the delivery, the power is in the word. And so, as we think about evangelism, we should spend time hearing afresh the word of Jesus. That's where the subtitle comes in: *Sharing Your Faith in 321*.

321 is a way of summarising the message of Jesus. You can read about it in an older book called *321* and a newer book called *How to See Life: A Guide in 321*. There's also a course which can be done in person or viewed online at 321course.com. 321 is all about 'life according to Jesus' and we'll be exploring it throughout these pages. I'd love you to hear the word again via 321 so that it beds down deeply in your heart and takes root. I want to evangelise you, so that you can evangelise others.

This book is therefore best used in conjunction with one of the 321 resources. And perhaps the best follow up to reading this book would be to put on a 321 course and invite your friends. But *How to Speak Life* can also stand alone, which is why I summarise the main ideas in each chapter.

As we begin, I want this book to be more than theoretical. Why not bring to mind two people you'd love to see come to Christ? To help you decide which two people to choose, consider who you might invite to a 321 course—whether in person or online? For every exercise we do in the book, keep these two people in mind and pray for them at the end of each chapter. Once you've worked through *How to Speak Life*, you might like to invite them either to church or to the 321 course, or both! In fact, why not pray for them right now.

I'M PRAYING FOR...

Name:

____

How would you describe their soil type?

____

____

____

Name:

____

How would you describe their soil type?

____

____

____

OK, ready? Let's learn how to speak life in 3, 2, 1…

321

JESUS: OUR GUIDE

CHAPTER 1

LOST IN SPACE

WHAT GETS YOU THINKING?

'LOST IN SPACE' IS EPISODE 1 OF THE 321 COURSE.

WATCH IT NOW

Alternatively read chapter 1 of *How to See Life: A Guide in 321*

WHAT'S THE STORY?

Picture this: Sasha wakes up on a space station with no memory of how she got there and no idea of who she is. Soon she meets two others: Hope and Doc. Hope is convinced it's going to be OK, she feels it in her bones: 'Someone out there is looking after us.' Doc is a scientist; he can't go by gut instinct. Instead he investigates the space craft and comes to a conclusion: the designer of the space craft exhibits great intelligence and care. There's probably purpose behind it all.

Sasha, though, is sceptical. She's unconvinced by Hope and her intuitions, and by Doc and his calculations. She thinks it would be far better if everyone shut up about *what's beyond the space craft*. Instead they should concentrate on making life on the ship as good as it can be.

> While the three debate, the space station shudders, a ship docks, the airlock opens and a man appears. Astonished, they ask 'Who are you?'
>
> 'I'm the rescue,' he says.
>
> His arrival changes everything.

THE BIG QUESTIONS

We come into this world with big questions: Who am I? What's the meaning of all this? Is there anything beyond this world?

These questions have been asked down through history. But different people have given different answers. 'Pre-modern people'—those before the scientific revolution of the 16th century—would be more like Hope. They are comfortable with spiritual answers. They would acknowledge a powerful realm beyond what we can see. For them the world is charged with meaning and they believe *there is more*. A lot of my friends are like Hope. They definitely believe in *something* even if they can't tell me what that something is, or how we can know. The Hope view of the world has never gone away. But in the last 500 years, another kind of view has become prominent.

Since the advent of the scientific revolution, 'modern people' have sought scientific answers. To discover the meaning of things, 'modern people' look within the world at what can be measured and tested. In the story of the space station, Doc represents this scientific view. He's different to Hope. Doc uses reason and experiment to answer the big questions. Having investigated the space craft he detects signs of a greater intelligence.

For the Docs of the world, life's biggest questions can be answered by studying nature. Your average Doc thinks scientific explanations provide the deepest, truest, most satisfying answers. A lot of my friends are like Doc. But then I have other friends too, like Sasha.

Sasha represents 'post-modern people'. She's wary of the spiritual truth claims of Hope *and* of the scientific truth claims of Doc. When she hears them going on about 'the true nature of the space craft' and 'what's beyond', she rolls her eyes. *We just don't know!*

The Sashas of the world are sceptical. When people presume to know the meaning of all things, a 'Sasha' will suspect that it's all a big power play. Instead of worrying about 'what's beyond', they'd rather get on and live as best they can in the here and now. A lot of my friends are post-modern like Sasha. In fact, a lot of *me* is like Sasha.

How about you, which way do you lean? We all have a natural temperament. What about the two friends you're praying for? Do they follow their hearts or their heads? Or maybe they don't feel they can trust either?

The point of the allegory is that your friends can be any of these characters—pre-modern, modern or post-modern—

but their need is exactly the same. It's the arrival of *Jesus* that's the game changer. When the rescuer appears, he doesn't really conform to anyone's expectations—not the spiritual, the scientific or the sceptical. Nor does he take a side in their debates. He completely changes the conversation. Now all the questions boil down to a single issue: *Can I trust this man?*

This is the way Jesus confronts the whole world. He is equally for the spiritual, the scientific and the sceptical. He also equally baffles the spiritual, the scientific and the sceptical! When I consider how to finish the *Lost in Space* story, I can't help imagining an ending in which Hope and Doc resist the rescuer but, almost in spite of herself, Sasha finds herself taking his hand. Why not? Jesus really is a game changer and when people encounter him, lives turn around.

That's our privilege as Christians: to introduce others to this man. The heart of evangelism is simply pointing to Jesus as the 'rescuer from beyond' who makes sense of it all. What our friends do with him is out of our hands, but making the introduction is our mission and our privilege. In this book I want to help you do that. You might feel that such a task is far beyond you. It is. But we're not alone as we introduce people to Jesus. We have his Spirit, his people, his Scriptures and a raft of encouragements that I'll highlight as we go. Here's the first help when we consider evangelism, and it's a biggy…

THIS IS JESUS' WORLD

Over the last 2,000 years the Apostle John has introduced more people to Jesus than perhaps any other human being! How has he accomplished such impressive evangelism? By telling the Jesus story and by doing it in cosmic perspective:

> *In the beginning was the Word, and the Word was with God, and the Word was God. He was with God in the beginning. Through him all things were made; without him nothing was made that has been made. In him was life, and that life was the light of all mankind.*
> **JOHN 1:1–4**

John's evangelism begins the way the universe begins: with Jesus! According to John, Jesus didn't just invent a religion, he invented the cosmos—together with his Father and the Holy Spirit. This is *Jesus'* world, a place shaped by his personality (v3), enlivened by his life (v4) and enlightened by his light (v9). When we introduce people to Jesus we are not introducing them to a Stranger, we are introducing them to the Landlord!

We might, then, need to adjust the *Lost in Space* allegory. In the story of Hope, Doc and Sasha, they wake up on a space station—an alien place. And the rescuer must also break in from outside. But in the story of our lives, we are born into *Jesus'* world. We are confronted by the reality of

Jesus every moment. In fact, it's a little bit like being born in the Jerusalem temple.

Imagine the Holy Place of Solomon's temple is all you've ever known. You're surrounded by architecture, ornaments, furniture and images dripping with spiritual significance. There's the table of the Bread of the Presence; there's the sevenfold lamp stand; there are the cherubim woven into the temple curtain. But imagine you've never been told the true significance of all these. You use the table for ping pong; you pretend the lamp stand is a trident; you play Pokémon with the cherubim—*gotta catch them all!* You live in a giant, multi-media presentation of the Lord and all his ways, but you've missed its true meaning. Until a friend comes along and begins to explain.

That's what evangelism is like. Our friends and family may not know Jesus but, whether they're a Hope, Doc or Sasha, they're living in his house and bumping up against his reality in a thousand different ways. They are, no doubt, misconstruing the meaning behind these things. But they don't live in neutral space. All things have been made through Jesus. Though the world is fallen, and though we are blinded by our sin, still all things bear Christ's imprint.

I find this hugely encouraging. When I'm daunted by the task of introducing my friends to Jesus, I remind myself: the whole *world* is on my side!

Years ago the BBC had a show called *Through the Keyhole*. Contestants would be shown selected footage of a celebrity's house and they'd have to guess whose house it was. After more and more clues, the contestants finally got it, but usually it had to be made pretty obvious. Evangelism is like this. Our friends see features of this world and they might think that 'this house' belongs to chance or fate or Allah or no one at all. Our privilege is to do the big reveal. We get to tell them: it's *Jesus'* house, and that's what makes sense of everything that had formerly intrigued and baffled them.

Here's one way to do that: it's our first 'seed to scatter'.

SEED TO SCATTER 1:
WHAT GETS YOU THINKING?

Every day we encounter things in Jesus' world designed to point us to him. What is it for you? It might be the beauty of the night sky or the ache in our hearts. It could be the joys of a newborn child or the sorrow of losing a loved one. Every now and then something makes us think—really think—about whether there's more going on in life than the daily grind.

SPEND SOME TIME CONSIDERING YOUR OWN ANSWERS. YOU MAY WANT TO JOT DOWN SOME THOUGHTS HERE...

What makes you ask the big questions about life, meaning and purpose?

____

____

____

____

____

____

What about your friends? Ask them!

The 'what gets you thinking seed' is about opening up the conversation to spiritual things. We're just being curious about our friends' outlook on life. Are there life events or features of the world that make them ask bigger questions, like what it's all about?

One way you can tap into this area is asking: 'Have you ever had a religious experience?' We might shy away from that terminology in church, but my friends and neighbours know what we mean. If I ask this, very often someone will tell me of an awe-inspiring moment or a significant life-event. Or they will simply launch into a TED talk summarising their life philosophy. At that point there are fruitful avenues for discussion everywhere. You can continue being curious, probing *why* certain things are so significant for them.

Perhaps when they tell you about the birth of a child or the death of a parent, you can think together about what makes those moments so significant. What does it say about life, ourselves, the meaning of it all?

You can ask them their history with these values: 'Have you always thought like that?' You can resonate with their likes and dislikes. And perhaps at some point you can give your own views about what gets *you* thinking. For me it would be things like:

- **LIFE.** Holding my firstborn in my arms thinking: How can there be a whole new *person* in the world? She wasn't here earlier, now she is. How can there be a new consciousness—a new being to love and be loved. And my goodness how much love!
- **MINDS.** We have the saying 'mind over matter', and it's true isn't it? Matter—physical stuff—*isn't* the most important thing. Minds are more important. Even if someone thinks matter is the most important thing—even if they think matter is everything!—that's a *thought* they're having.

And thoughts aren't material. What are they exactly? It's so hard to say. We're in the realm of deep mystery here.

- **MUSIC.** I mean, come on! Music! I'm chugging along in this work-a-day world and then, all of a sudden, my soul vibrates with the frequency of this primeval power, this thrumming glory, this expansive and ineffable beauty. How can sound waves do this to us?

There are all sorts of things that spring to mind when I consider 'what gets me thinking'. And you can tell that I get quite animated about this stuff. I'll express my interests in a me-shaped way. You will express your interests in a you-shaped way. But you have interests. You too have likes and goals and ultimate values that inspire you. And so do your friends.

IT BEGAN WITH A FACEBOOK VIDEO

'Woah,' said my neighbour, his eyes glistening as he stood on his porch, phone in one hand, cigarette in the other.

'What's that?' I asked. He went back to the beginning of the video and played it for me: the story of an American High Schooler with a developmental disability. The teenager loved basketball but never got to play—until the last few minutes of the final game of the season. The coach put him on and the home crowd willed him to score. But he missed, and then missed, and then missed again. With just seconds left, the opposition handed him the ball and when he scored, the cheer nearly lifted the roof. They rushed the court and carried the kid on their shoulders on multiple laps of honour.

Now we both had tears in our eyes. 'I *love* those stories,' I said.

And then we talked about other videos it reminded us of. Like the videos where a homeless person is given money which they then pass on to someone even more needy. Or like the people born deaf who get cochlear implants and you watch as they hear for the first time. And we cry maybe more for these strangers than we do for the situations in our own lives.

'What's that about?' asked my friend. And whether it was a rhetorical question or not, I chose to answer it.

'It's compassion. It's supernatural,' I said. 'The whole natural world runs on "survival of the fittest"—and the sacrifice of the weakest. It's dog eat dog and it's depressing. But then you get something like this where the weak are protected and the little guy is lifted up and if feels so different.' We went on to talk about how *super*-natural it is when we see the people on top serving others. We got on to how this is an echo of the Jesus story—how Jesus 'the highest' came down to be sacrificed, so we, the lowest, can be raised up.

We chatted about lots of other things that day too, but that Sunday he started coming to church with me. He's still coming two years later. And it all began with a video about kindness.

This is Jesus' world.

QUESTIONS FOR REFLECTION

- How does it help our evangelism to know that this is Jesus' world?
- How do you answer the question, *What gets you thinking?*
- How might your friends answer that question?
- How do those things relate to Jesus?

321

CHAPTER 2

THE GREATEST STORY EVER TOLD

THAT'S WHAT I LOVE ABOUT JESUS

'THE GREATEST STORY EVER TOLD' IS EPISODE 2 OF THE 321 COURSE.

WATCH IT NOW

Alternatively read chapter 2 of *How to See Life: A Guide in 321*

WHAT'S THE STORY?

Picture this: *The greatest story ever told.* What springs to mind? If you had to write 'the story of stories', what would you come up with? Perhaps it would be some kind of Hero's Journey involving struggle, sacrifice and victory against the odds.

Probably you'd end up writing some version of the Jesus story. That's because you cannot improve on the Jesus story. Every dimension of it maxes out. You could not have a greater hero (Christ, our Maker) descend to a lower depth (the cross) to have a wider effect (the whole world) for a greater duration (eternity).

As Paul says, 'how wide and long and high and deep is the love of Christ' (Ephesians 3:18)! From one perspective it's little wonder that the Jesus story has taken over the world. It is unimprovable. From another perspective, it's very surprising indeed.

> After all, Jesus dies as a despised criminal in his early 30s, in a small province crushed by the mighty empire of Rome. Within three centuries, though, that empire will call him Lord and he will become the world's most influential figure, splitting history in two, and spawning the greatest movement of people on the planet.

PROVE IT!

'What would make you believe in God?' I asked.

My friend, let's call him Matt, had clearly heard the question before and answered instantly, saying, 'If God rearranged the stars in the sky to spell out the Ten Commandments, then I'd believe.'

I don't know where your friends and neighbours set the bar for 'proof of God', but Matt set his to galactic heights. How should I respond? My first thought was to point to the current arrangement of the stars. It's Jesus' world after all. The heavens are already miraculously well ordered. You can Google 'the fine tuning of the cosmos' and you will see that the physical constants of this universe had to be *just so* in order to permit life.

Incredibly, and against near infinite odds, the stars are part of a life-sustaining universe. If we truly appreciated the astonishing order of the universe we would consider 'messages in the stars' to be a cheap parlour trick, distracting us from the gargantuan wonder of life pressing in on us from every angle.

But a second answer occurred to me. I simply asked him, 'Would you like such a God?'

'What do you mean?" Matt said.

'Well, would you *like* the kind of God who shuffles around galaxies all to spell out THOU SHALT NOT?'

He answered forcefully: 'No! I could never like God. But if he proved his existence I'd admit I was wrong.' At this point we found common ground. I said I agreed with him entirely. The God Matt was describing was not a God I wanted to believe in either.

But with Jesus... now there's a different kind of God altogether.

HOW FAITH HAPPENS

I'd love Matt to trust in Jesus. We all desperately want our family and friends to believe. It's essential that they do. But how's that going to happen? How does faith in Jesus come about?

Many see faith as a muscle to flex, as though someone can screw up their abs, grunt, and force themselves to believe. If faith works like this, evangelism would essentially be about forcing people, or commanding people, or cajoling people, or daring people, or bribing people to have faith. 'Just do it,' we would cry. But this isn't how faith works. Or people! Faith is not a thing we push out of ourselves via willpower. Instead faith is pulled out of us by something external—by something best described as 'glory'. Allow me to illustrate.

Imagine the conversation between a father and his son, Dutiful Derek. The father says 'We're going on holiday to Switzerland and we'll watch the sun rise over the snow-capped Alps—you will be awe-struck.'

'Do I *have* to be awe-struck?' Dutiful Derek says.

The father replies, 'Umm, well, it's not so much a case of "have to", but when you see the view, awe will strike!'

Derek sighs deeply. 'If I must.'

Later his father says, 'Derek, one day you're going to meet a girl who will steal your heart and you'll fall in love.'

'Do I *have* to fall in love?'

'Derek, it's the best feeling in the world! You spend time with the right girl and it just sort of happens, whoosh!'

'OK, I guess I'll try my best.'

Of course, when Derek sees sunrise over the Swiss Alps, he simply *is* awe-struck. When he meets the right girl, he *does* fall in love. But how tragic it would be if Derek sits in church, Sunday by Sunday, seeing the glory of Jesus but feeling like faith is his *duty*. The beautiful view, the beautiful woman, *and* the beautiful Saviour are all alike. They have a glory to them that we need to see. Once seen, this glory will draw from us the correct response. If we remain simply dutiful, we must be blind to the glory.

John, our favourite evangelist, is like Derek's dad driving us to the Swiss Alps and saying 'Get a load of the view!' We cannot make our friends believe any more than Derek's dad could make Derek's jaw drop. But a good evangelist points and says 'Look!' That's what John does throughout his Gospel.

THE GLORY OF JESUS

John tells us from firsthand experience what it was like to clap eyes on the 'Word made flesh'. It was glorious (John 1:14)!

In the Hebrew language of the Old Testament, the word 'glory' conjures up images of weightiness, gravity and substance. In the New Testament the word shows up often in the context of light, of brightness—of a shining brilliance. The glory of God is the God-ness of God—the thing that makes him who he is. If there's an echo of his glory in the Swiss Alps or the experience of falling in love, what must it be like to *see* the uncreated Original?

Such glory outshines everything else. It attracts our attention, our love, our very self. It draws faith from us like iron filings flying to an electromagnet. No wonder John shapes his whole Gospel around revealing the glory of Jesus.

> *What Jesus did here in Cana of Galilee was the first of the signs through which he revealed his glory; and his disciples believed in him.* **JOHN 2:11**

This is how John's Gospel works. And faith. And people! When we see something trustworthy, we find ourselves trusting. And so the first half of John's Gospel (often called 'the book of signs') points us to the grace and truth of Jesus in mending our broken world. Then, after chapter 12, we reach the second half of John (often called 'the book of glory'). This is all about his death. And listen to the way Jesus describes it:

> *'The hour has come for the Son of Man to be glorified. … Now my soul is troubled, and what shall I say? "Father, save me from this hour"? No, it was for this very reason I came to this hour. Father, glorify your name!'*
>
> *Then a voice came from heaven, 'I have glorified it, and will glorify it again.' The crowd that was there and heard it said it had thundered; others said an angel had spoken to him.*
>
> *Jesus said, 'This voice was for your benefit, not mine. Now is the time for judgment on this world; now the prince of this world will be driven out. And I, when I am lifted up from the earth, will draw all people to myself.' He said this to show the kind of death he was going to die.*
> **JOHN 12:23, 27–33**

Here is a strange and awesome combination of ideas: 'hour', 'glory' and '*death*'! Before in John's Gospel, Jesus spoke of his 'hour' as the time he would be 'lifted up' (John 3:14; 8:28). His followers might have imagined him being lifted up on a stage or a throne. But now we see the quintessence of his glory. He will be lifted up on the cross. This demonstrates his true God-ness. And this is what will attract the world.

From one point of view it's absurd. How can 'death by torture' be in any sense attractive—to anyone? From another point of view, this is 'the glorification of the glory of God' as Mike Reeves puts it.[1] As the Son he has shared for eternity in the glorious life of God. As our Maker he gloriously gave life *to* the world. But at the cross, Jesus our Redeemer gives his life *for* the world. It is the ultimate demonstration of 'grace and truth'.

On Good Friday, Jesus tells the truth about humanity. For him to meet us where we are, he had to enter godforsakenness—'hell on earth'. If we hadn't realised it before, looking at the cross shows us we really are in trouble. This is a sobering truth. But if we take a second look, we'll discover incredible grace. On the cross we see a Saviour so committed to making his dwelling with us that no price is too great. In love he *wants* to meet us, even if that means curse and judgement. The lifting up of Jesus

---

1 Michael Reeves, *How to Enjoy God (Matters of the Heart, Part 1)*, online audio recording, 2011, <https://www.unionpublishing.org/resource/matters-of-the-heart-1-how-to-enjoy-god-michael-reeves/> [accessed 27 February 2024].

on the cross attracts faith. And so does his raising up on the third day—though there's a famous doubter who holds out for a week.

For a week, Thomas refuses to believe (John 20:24–29). Then he meets the risen Jesus. He sees his battle scars—those war wounds that prove Jesus' suffering love—and faith flies from his awe-struck heart: 'My Lord and my God!' That's the power of the glory of Jesus.

At this point, many complain: *It's all well and good for Thomas but my friends aren't going to get a resurrection appearance to make them believe.* But listen to how the story unfolds. Jesus tells Thomas that people are 'blessed… who have not seen and yet have believed' (John 20:29). If we wonder how that's ever going to happen, John tells us:

> *Jesus performed many other signs in the presence of his disciples, which are not recorded in this book. But these are written that you may believe that Jesus is the Messiah, the Son of God, and that by believing you may have life in his name.* **JOHN 20:30–31**

John's Gospel—in fact, the whole Bible—is written so that people might believe. We have the Jesus story in black and white for all time. Through it we have 'seen' the glory of Christ—his grace and truth. And countless billions have found themselves believing in him.

SEED TO SCATTER 2:

THAT'S WHAT I LOVE ABOUT JESUS

Much of my evangelism involves me responding to questions and objections with, 'Yeah, good point, I don't know. But what do you make of Jesus?'

When people ask me about suffering, while there are many true biblical things to say, I usually find myself replying:

> *'I don't know. All I know is that God came to earth and suffered, so God and suffering can't be opposites. I mean that's what I love about Jesus: on the cross, he suffered the most, so he gives us a unique perspective on God and suffering. What do you make of him?'*

People ask me about judgement and how a loving God can send people to hell, and again I point back to Jesus:

> *'There's a thousand things about judgement I don't know, but one thing the Bible tells me is who the Judge is. It's Jesus. And I love it in the Gospels when I see him blasting the lofty and lifting up the lowly. I reckon this is the one Person who can be trusted with the job. What do you make of him?'*

When people ask me about the hypocrisy of the church, I end up saying things like:

> *'The people of Jesus have often been unChristlike. We can be horrendously hypocritical—not because we're*

> *Christian, but because we're human and humans are rubbish like that. But I keep coming back to Jesus himself. You can accuse the church of a lot of wickedness (just like you can accuse all humans of wickedness). But—this is what I love about Jesus—none of those charges stick to him! What do you make of that?'*

Check out the FAQs in *How to See Life: A Guide in 321* for more answers to hard questions, but whether our friends believe in God or not, whether they've clapped eyes on a Bible or not, whatever objections they might have to Christian faith, it's Jesus they need to encounter. Let's make sure our evangelism revolves around him.

SPEND SOME TIME CONSIDERING YOUR OWN ANSWERS. YOU MAY WANT TO JOT DOWN SOME THOUGHTS HERE...

What do you love about Jesus? What aspect of his grace and truth particularly grab you? Have you got favourite examples from the Gospels?

____

____

____

____

____

LEARNING FROM THE EVANGELISTS

Just like John (and Matthew, Mark and Luke), the most helpful thing we can do in evangelism is to show Jesus to our friends and family. Here are three things we can learn from the Gospel writers:

Firstly, let's read them! When John says 'these are written that you may believe' (John 20:31), he really does mean *you*. The noun 'you' is plural and the verb 'believe' is present continuous. It's about believers going on believing—something we desperately need.

Sometimes in evangelism training I ask a room full of Christians 'Who needs to hear the gospel?' Immediately the answers ring out: 'Everyone!' 'The world!' Of course. Perfect answers. Then, as I wait for more ideas, people think further: 'The lost', 'Those who haven't heard' and so on. Then someone gets the idea and tentatively suggests: 'Christians?' Finally I say: 'All of the above, but first of all, *me*!' I need to hear the gospel.

In a similar vein, I'll often ask this question: 'What do we need to do with the gospel?' Once again it's a trap (I'm awful, I know). People answer: 'Share it!' 'Preach it!' 'Take it to the nations!' They're at an evangelism seminar, after all.

But soon they get it. *Evangel*-ism is about promoting the evangel (i.e. the gospel). And what do we need to do with the gospel? Firstly, *hear it. Receive it. Believe it. Rejoice in it.*

Jesus said 'the mouth speaks from the overflow of the heart' (Matthew 12:34, HCSB). If our words of witness have dried up, Jesus diagnoses a heart condition. But there's also a remedy: fill your heart with the glory of Jesus. Look to Christ again. Allow his glory to produce faith once again. As we fill up on Jesus, words will follow. They might not be impressive words but they will come from exactly the right place.

Secondly, we should *use* them! For the better part of 2,000 thousand years people have been encountering Christ through the Gospels. Dutiful Dereks and Doubting Thomases from around the world have 'seen' the glory of Christ and found themselves confessing: 'My Lord and my God!' In terms of effective evangelism it's impossible to think of a better tool. What we have in the Gospels are the Spirit-inspired biographies of Jesus. If we want our friends and families to encounter Jesus we should encourage our friends to engage with them in every way possible.

I'm constantly asking people, 'Have you read a Gospel—a biography of Jesus—since becoming an adult?' I advise them, 'Crack open a Gospel and shoot up a prayer, saying: *Jesus, show me who you really are.'*

I invite people to Bible studies. Resources like the Word 121 are made for this kind of thing, designed to help you take a friend through John's Gospel (see theWord121.com). I've written a reading plan for John's Gospel for Bible.com and the app YouVersion (bible.com/r/AR4). It takes people through, a chapter at a time. I invite people to courses like

321 that are extended meditations on the Gospels. And I invite them to church to hear more from the Bible.

And thirdly, we should *follow* the Gospels. We can aim at what they aim for. In other words, our goal should be the same as that of Matthew, Mark, Luke and John. We too can tell stories of Jesus, showing off his glory—his grace and his truth.

There's little we can do to change human hearts and, to be honest, there's little that our friends can do to change their own hearts. But, as we paint biblical portraits of Christ, *he* can draw people to himself. The most attractive man who's ever lived—a man who has in fact attracted more of a following than anyone else in history—*is* glorious. We don't have to make him glorious. We don't have to embellish the story. We simply have to point to him and, when he is lifted up, he 'will draw all people to' himself (John 12:32).

QUESTIONS FOR REFLECTION

- How did faith in Jesus happen in your own life? Can you see the ways in which the 'glory of Jesus' drew faith out of you?
- How do you finish the sentence, *That's what I love about Jesus…?*
- When it comes to the Gospels, what will help you read them, use them and follow them?
- How might your evangelism benefit from being more *Jesus*-focused?

321

GOD'S THREE-NESS

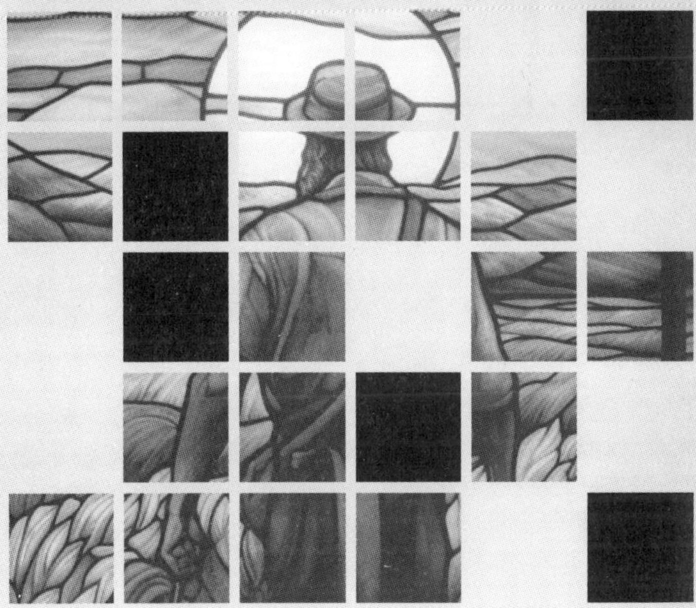

CHAPTER 3

SAVING PRIVATE PHILIPS

WHICH GOD DO(N'T) YOU BELIEVE IN?

'SAVING PRIVATE PHILIPS' IS EPISODE 3 OF THE 321 COURSE.

WATCH IT NOW

Alternatively read chapter 3 of *How to See Life: A Guide in 321*

WHAT'S THE STORY?

Picture this: Private Philips, a soldier in World War 2, is bleeding out from his wounds. As he faces 'meeting his Maker', he has one final question for the chaplain: 'Is God really like Jesus?'

This true story was told often by the chaplain in question, Tom Torrance. The answer he gave that morning comforted Philips in his final moments. It's also something Torrance reflected upon for the rest of his life. Here is a truth to carry you through life and death: God is entirely and eternally the Jesus-God.

THE JESUS–GOD

She came to every session and sat in the front row, taking copious notes. I was speaking at Exeter University and this one woman seemed more engrossed than anyone else. She came from Iran and was in the UK, ostensibly, to complete a Master's degree in law. But her real passion was studying the Bible. A few years earlier an uncle had sidled up to her at a wedding and recommended she read the Gospels (he had recently, and secretly, become a Christian). Despite being a teenager in a devout Muslim home she managed to get a copy and read it each night under the covers.

She told me she was captivated by the person of Jesus as she read through Matthew and then Mark. Halfway through Luke's Gospel, she came to this conclusion: 'God cannot be the God of the Ayatollahs. He must be the Jesus-God.' The Ayatollahs are the religious authorities in Iran. These Muslim leaders had proclaimed a vision of God which she now recognised to be false. Their God was not worthy of the name. But in looking at Jesus, she concluded: *he is!*

She got it. Jesus is 'the Word of the Father' as we saw in the introduction. If you were to imagine a cartoon of John 1 you might picture a throne representing the power and authority of God with a massive speech bubble coming from it, basically filling the whole frame. And what's inside the speech bubble? It's not a text, a command, or a poem, it's a person. *Jesus himself* is 'the Word of God'. *He* is what God is saying. He is what God has always been saying.

That's why, in the story of Saving Private Philips, Tom Torrance was able to comfort the young soldier. When Philips asked 'Is God really like Jesus?' the chaplain answered:

> *The only God that there is, [is] the God who [has] come to us in Jesus, shown his face to us, and poured out his love to us as our Saviour.*[2]

Here are words to comfort the dying—*and* the living: the Jesus-God is the only God that there is. We should not imagine any God who is different from the One we meet in Jesus. God *really* is like Jesus because Jesus is forever God's Word, Wisdom, Image, Radiance and Representation (John 1:1; 1 Corinthians 1:30; Colossians 1:15; Hebrews 1:3). Here's one way I often put it: Jesus is completely and utterly God-sized and, at the same time, God is completely and utterly Jesus-shaped.

I say this because our temptation is to think the opposite. We often imagine Jesus to be less than divine and to think of God as less than 'Christ-like'. But no, the Father and Son are so united that they are 'in' one another (John 14:11, 20). What you see in Jesus is what you get with God.

Once we grasp this, we have incredible assurance. We also have something else: a profound window onto the doctrine of the Trinity.

THE TRUTH OF THE THREE

Often we think of trinitarian theology as something off to one side in the Christian life. We certainly don't consider it central to evangelism. Instead we might assume that it's

2 Alister McGrath, *T. F. Torrance: An Intellectual Biography* (T&T Clarke, 2006), p. 74.

about ticking some doctrinal boxes or offering our friends analogies of 'three-ness'. It's really not. It's all about focusing hearts and minds on the Jesus-God.

When we realise that only the Jesus-God is God, we realise that Jesus and the Father have exactly the same *nature*. But—and this is crucial for the truth of THREE—they are not the same *person*. Jesus is very obviously *sent* by the Father and *empowered* by the Spirit. Jesus, the Father and the Spirit are THREE distinct persons. But the THREE are one. How should we understand this? And how can we help our friends to understand it?

Consider how Jesus is most fully described in the Gospels (see also Mark 1:1, Mark 14:61 and Matthew 16:16):

> *...Jesus is the Messiah, the Son of God...* **JOHN 20:31**

As the Son of God, Jesus is the Father's beloved. As the Messiah (or Christ), he's the Anointed One—filled to overflowing with the Spirit (see Psalm 45:6–7; Luke 4:18).

Whenever the Gospel writers introduce Jesus as 'the Messiah, the Son of God', we are being shown two things at once: there are THREE persons and they are utterly united. It's clear that the persons are distinct—when you view Jesus' baptism, or listen to his teaching, or hear him pray, it's obvious that the Father is a different person from Christ, and so is the Spirit. But it's also obvious that when you meet Jesus, you are introduced immediately to his Father and to his Spirit (John 14:7,16–18). That's because this THREE-personed God is one.

Put all this together and we get the central truth of the THREE in 321:

> *God is a loving union of THREE: the Father, the Son and the Holy Spirit.*

In the FAQs I expand some more on the crucial need for trinitarian theology in our evangelism. But none of this is to tie our friends in philosophical knots. It's about introducing them to Jesus—the Spirit-filled Son of the Father. And when they've seen *him*, they've encountered the fullness of God.

'IF GOD'S NOT LIKE JESUS...'

While our kids fed the ducks at the park, my friend Carrie asked what I was doing the next day. I said I was preaching in the morning.

'My grandfather was a preacher,' she said. I had no idea. Carrie usually kept her spiritual cards very close to her chest. 'Yeah, he was a unitarian minister,' she continued, looking to see my approval or otherwise.

'Really!' I replied. 'Man, that's one thing I could never understand: believing in God but not in Jesus.' This caught her off guard.

'But isn't the Jesus thing harder to believe than... like, a Higher Power? I can understand a Higher Power, it's all the Jesus and Bible stuff that makes it tricky.'

'I'm the opposite,' I said. 'I grew up thinking God was like electricity—a power you could use for your benefit or who'd zap you if you got on the wrong side of him. I believed in the Electricity God but could never warm to him. It's when I read the Gospels and met Jesus that I saw a God with a personality—a God who loves and laughs and shouts and cries. I always liked what Lord Byron said: "If God's not like Jesus, he ought to be."'

'Huh!' she exclaimed, looking like she was really processing things.

'Oh yeah,' I said, 'but if God *is* like Jesus, I'm in—you know?'

Like my friend Carrie, many people *think* they understand who God is. They think the idea of God is obvious. Even if they disbelieve in God, they're pretty sure they know what they're disbelieving. But John says if we cut Jesus out of the picture, we're no longer considering the real God:

> *No one has ever seen God; the only God, who is at the Father's side, he has made him known.* **JOHN 1:18, ESV**

This verse is revolutionary, upending our natural thinking. It tells us starkly that humanity does not naturally know God. It's only Jesus who reveals him. It's Jesus who is on show to the world—the eternal Word of God who happens to be the most famous man who ever lived (talk about a public figure!). It's Jesus our friends need to see if they're to know God. And so we need to define terms.

LET'S GET SPECIFIC

I have some unhelpful prejudices when it comes to evangelism. I'm prone to thinking my atheist friends are harder to evangelise than those who believe in 'God'. I see them as doubly lost, because *they don't even believe in God*. On the other hand I think of friends who do believe in God as 'nearly there'. It's stupid, but I have this gut feeling that all I need to do is convince them that *Jesus* is the 'God' they already believe in and—hey presto—they've arrived.

But that approach won't convert my friend to Jesus. Instead, it will convert Jesus into a false God—in their minds, I mean! I'll be trying to squeeze Jesus into a mould he doesn't fit—making him like the 'God' they imagine. I should be doing the opposite. I should be letting Jesus break the mould of *everyone's* thinking—whether they call themselves an atheist, a theist, a Muslim or even a Christian. Jesus needs to be shaping our thinking *and* our conversations. The simplest way I've found to do this is to steal Tom Wright's question.

Tom Wright has been a bishop, a professor and the author of over 70 books. In the 1990s he was chaplain of Worcester College, Oxford. Many students would tell him not to bother trying to convert them because they didn't believe in God. Tom Wright had a great reply: 'Oh that's interesting, which God is it you don't believe in?'

The student would be taken aback but when pushed would eventually describe some kind of distant individual, far away—high on power, low on personality—a Zeus figure with a thunderbolt ready to hurl. And what did Tom Wright say to those students? 'You're right not to believe in that God, I don't believe in that God either. Let me tell you about the God I see revealed in Jesus.' It's a game changer! It is so powerful to come alongside the atheist in their unbelief, to share their disdain for the Tyrant they've imagined, and then to point them to the unparalleled glory of Jesus.

All this should make us much more eager to go beneath the surface in our faith conversations. If people tell us they believe in God, even if they tell us they're a Christian, there's a time and a place to question them. You don't have to be rude about it. I don't recommend you poke them in the chest and cry: 'Prove you're a *real* Christian! Show me your fish bumper sticker!' But there is such a thing as 'nominal Christianity', that is: Christianity in name only. And if you want a deep conversation you'll want to go beneath the 'Christian' label.

The same is true if someone uses the 'atheist' or 'agnostic' label. In some times and places 'Christianity' has functioned as an unthinking label that you adopt for convenience. But at other times and places (the modern, secular West, for instance!), 'atheist' or 'agnostic' can function in a similar way. I see it everywhere. Faith will come up in conversation and my friend will declare their 'atheist' label. But it's worth going deeper. Sometimes a self-identified atheist can quote Richard Dawkins chapter and verse. But far more often it's a cultural marker rather than a heartfelt conviction. In other words there is such a thing as nominal atheism. And the answer to nominal atheism is pretty much the same as the answer to nominal Christianity. You say 'That's interesting, what do you make of Jesus?'

Whether a person is young or old, whether they identify as Christian, atheist, agnostic, Hindu or Jedi Knight, we need to get back to basics and ask a much more foundational question: *which* God are we talking about? That brings us to our seed to scatter for this chapter.

SEED TO SCATTER 3:

WHICH GOD DO(N'T) YOU BELIEVE IN?

If your friend believes in God, ask them 'Which God do you believe in?' Or if that way of framing things sounds too alien, ask them to describe God. What is he/she/it like? How does this God relate to us and to the world? Has this God done anything? Does this God want anything? How do you feel about such a God? How does this God feel about you? Get them to elaborate.

If your friend doesn't believe in God, ask them 'Which God don't you believe in?' And try to get as specific as possible. You will almost certainly find common ground with your atheist friend. You will probably find yourself agreeing that the 'God' they mistrust you also mistrust. But there's something unique about Jesus.

This question—Which God do(n't) you believe in?—is brilliant at clearing the path for a Jesus conversation. Having considered the selfish Gods of this world, or the distant Gods, or the grandfather in the sky Gods, the contrast with the Jesus-God is immense.

SPEND SOME TIME CONSIDERING YOUR OWN ANSWERS. YOU MAY WANT TO JOT DOWN SOME THOUGHTS HERE...

What false pictures of God are you personally prone to imagine? How could you explain these in language your friends would understand?

How would you describe the uniqueness of the Jesus-God? What phrases, stories, illustrations would you use?

What difference has it made to your life to think of God in a properly *Christian* way?

ANSWERING OBJECTIONS

In this chapter I've been insisting that we focus our 'God conversations' on the Jesus-God. Let's not get lost in generic God-talk. Let's speak of Christ. I think this approach has immense benefits. But of course, it also opens us up to an obvious objection: 'Why limit yourself only to Jesus? Can't we get what Jesus is offering *elsewhere*?' As we round off this chapter, let's consider something that our friends might find *really* off-putting: the exclusivity of Christ.

To do that, I'll make the objection as difficult as possible. Here are perhaps the three starkest verses in the New Testament that declare it's *only* Jesus who can save:

- In John 14:6, Jesus says, 'I am the way and the truth and the life. No one comes to the Father except through me.'
- In Ephesians 2:12, Paul says those who are 'separate from Christ' are 'without hope and without God in the world'.
- In Acts 4:12, Peter says of Jesus, 'Salvation is found in no one else, for there is no other name under heaven given to mankind by which we must be saved.'

According to these verses, there is no Father, no hope and no salvation apart from Jesus. This might sound outrageously narrow. But here's my plea: press in—the exclusivity of Jesus is good news. Because apart from Jesus, no one is actually offering what he's offering. (Cults such as Mormonism and the Jehovah's Witnesses might sound like they get close, but they offer a distorted view of Jesus and therefore a distorted view of salvation.)

Let's first think of 'coming to the Father'.

My Iranian friend grew up knowing there are 99 names for Allah. 'Father' is not one of them. For a Muslim to imagine Allah as a Father would be, for them, a terrible blasphemy. In other religions, there might be a select few children of the gods, but they are heroes of renown, not regular believers. And of course in atheism there is no Heavenly Father to know.

When you shop around in the worldview marketplace, you recognise that Christianity has a unique selling point: no one gets a Father except through Jesus. At that point the exclusivity of Jesus is attractive not repulsive. It's similar with Ephesians 2:12.

The hope which Jesus offers stands alone. In Islam, Muslims can have no assurance of their future, but paradise is the destination of the righteous (rather than a renewed earth, as in Christianity). In the karmic religions (e.g. Hinduism and Buddhism), the 'hope' is to dissolve into the ocean of being like a drop of water in the sea. In atheism, the heat death of the universe awaits. Contrast this with the hope Christ offers. He rose bodily and promises his people *and his planet* a similar pathway and future. This is another unique selling point, so to speak. No one else offers hope for our bodies and our world. And no one else offers salvation either.

When Peter says that salvation is only found in Jesus, it might sound bigoted but, once again, we need to browse the offerings of 'the competition'. Muslims don't speak of salvation. Allah doesn't save sinners, he rewards good Muslims. The karmic religions don't have salvation in anything like the sense the Bible speaks of—karma gives you what you deserve. Atheism certainly doesn't have a category for salvation. With atheism, everyone gets the same judgement. It's very egalitarian, but it's also merciless—we all get death forever.

Notice that these three offerings—the Father, hope and salvation—are about a unique vision for God, the world and you. Jesus offers us a unique picture of *God*: a Father who fills us with his Spirit. He offers us a unique picture of the *world*: hope beyond death. And he offers a unique picture of *you*: he saves you by making you one with him forever. It's an exclusive offer. But it's uniquely good!

The exclusivity of Jesus is not something to fear in evangelism. It's something to own. After all, why should our friends consider Christ if they can get what he's offering elsewhere? They can't, though. Not even remotely. They must come to Jesus. But as they do, they won't squeeze through a *little Jesus* towards something else. They'll find a *cosmic Jesus* offering something so vast that no one else even dares to promise it. Your friends will never meet anyone like Jesus. Let's make much of *him*.

QUESTIONS FOR REFLECTION

- How do the ideas of the Jesus-God and the Trinity fit together?
- How might your friends answer the question, *Which God do(n't) you believe in?*
- How would you finish this sentence, 'You won't find anyone like Jesus…'? What things might you talk about if discussing Christ's uniqueness?

CHAPTER 4

FROM HEAVEN WITH LOVE

THAT'S WHY I LIVE DIFFERENTLY

'FROM HEAVEN WITH LOVE' IS EPISODE 4 OF THE 321 COURSE.

WATCH IT NOW

Alternatively read chapter 4 of *How to See Life: A Guide in 321*

WHAT'S THE STORY?

Picture this: You discover a machine that rewinds the cosmic clock. It takes you back in time—before people, before planets, before protons. What do you imagine was there before the world began? In other words, how do you picture life 'in the beginning'?

A Christian has an utterly unique and spectacularly wonderful answer to that question: love.

EVERYBODY NEEDS SOMEBODY TO LOVE

Nowadays it's easy to listen to one song on repeat. Back when I was a student—in the 1900s—you had to stop your Sony Walkman and hit rewind. I was too stingy to buy a Sony Walkman, mine was a Phoney Walkman. I was also too stingy to waste precious battery life on something as frivolous as rewinding. So I would take out the cassette and twirl it around a pencil until I'd physically spooled the tape back to the beginning. Then I'd jam it back in and hit play, all because one song had captured me: 'Everybody Needs Somebody to Love'.

I had this signature song from *The Blues Brothers* soundtrack bouncing around my brain for most of my degree. For three years I'd been studying the towering thinkers of the last two and a half millennia: from ancient greats like Socrates, Plato and Aristotle to giants of the last 500 years like Descartes, Kant and Marx. But it was John Belushi who began burrowing into my heart. When he howled 'Everybody…' it resonated like nothing else. As human universals go, this made more sense than anything I'd studied: *Love! Of course!*

In my final year, Blur released their seven-and-a-half-minute epic, 'Tender'. To be fair, lyrically there's quite a lot of padding in those seven and a half minutes. The only line of substance is the one everyone remembers as Damon Albarn sings about the greatest thing we have—love. And for a philosophy student at the turn of the millennium it became the soundtrack to my conversion.

My friend had persisted for three years in inviting me to church. Eventually I relented, whereupon I hated the preacher, and then found myself returning, Sunday by Sunday, to hate him some more. And then I hated him some less. And then, reading the Gospels, it all fell into place: Love *is* the greatest thing… but not if we're purposeless sacks of meat. Love *is* the greatest thing… but only if love is actually at the heart of the cosmos. And only Christians can say that.

As I was reading through the Gospels I met Someone who claimed to be the Light and Logic of the cosmos. The Gospel writers—those original evangelists—were doing their work: presenting the glory of Jesus to the eyes of my heart. At some point I thought, 'Yep, that's it. *He's* it. *He's* the greatest thing. He's love. He's Lord. The songs are true!'

Suddenly Blur, The Blues Brothers, being, beauty and bliss—everything—made sense! It all clicked. And yet none of this works without the truth of THREE. All of this depends on God being Father, Son and Holy Spirit, united in love.

NOTHING, CHAOS, POWER OR LOVE

This chapter began with a thought experiment: What do we think was there 'in the beginning'? In *How to See Life: A Guide in 321,* I speak about four basic answers you can give to that question: nothing, chaos, power or love. These aren't hard and fast answers. There's also huge overlap. When you think about it, the scientific story of our origins is essentially a combination of the first three. Out of nothing—bang!—everything unfolds according to purposeless processes.

But what is glaring in its absence from this secular story is love. Therefore modern life is the attempt to build a meaningful existence out of the rubble of nothing, chaos and power. We love the idea of love—how can we not? But in the secular story, love only goes so deep. It's a surface level phenomenon, something that we generate in our better moments. But it wasn't there 'in the beginning', and it won't be there at the end.

In response to the barrenness of the secular vision, some of our friends and family might opt for a *religious* answer—enlisting 'God' to solve this crisis of meaning. But that move has only limited value. Remember our question from chapter 3: *Which God do(n't) you believe in?* There are many conceptions of 'God' that are basically indistinguishable from 'Power'. A solitary 'God' for instance is not love (for who would the Almighty Loner love before creation? Himself? That would be narcissism, not love). A cosmic Force or Energy is not love—it's not ultimately personal. Multiple gods are not united in love.

The only God that helps us here is the triune God—the loving union of THREE:

> *Father, I want those you have given me to be with me where I am, and to see my glory, the glory you have given me because you loved me before the creation of the world.* **JOHN 17:24**

John 17 is so rich it should come with a cholesterol warning. Before the creation of the world there was a Niagara Falls of love crashing down on the Son from the Father. This Father-Son love is older than the universe. It's more fundamental than physics, more crucial than chemistry, more basic than biology. If you could wind back the clock on the cosmos you could never get back before love. Love is primordial. Love is something God never had to create because God *is* love.

That's how John put it in his first letter—twice in fact—*God is love* (1 John 4:8,16). He doesn't just say that God is lov*ing*. That would be true but completely insufficient to describe what John has in mind. God *is* love: fundamentally; constitutionally; eternally.

This means we have come from love, been shaped by love, and are intended for love. In evangelism this is an immense truth for our non-Christian friends to grasp. But it's also vital for the church. Because our embrace of this love is the very heartbeat of our mission.

TWO MODELS FOR MISSION

Have you ever thought to yourself something like... *Christianity is shrinking in the West, our pews are empty, our influence has gone, our time is running out... we need to gain converts!* This is an emptiness mentality. And it runs to the world in order to find fullness. I'm going to call this model: 'Up and In' evangelism.

Fundamentally it's a mission born of need. Evangelism involves bold missionaries holding their noses and dashing out into the big, bad world to snatch a few people from perdition. We pluck them *up* from the world and extract them from life in the here and now. We bring them *in* to a small, insular community defined in opposition to all that's beyond. The world is a sinking ship and evangelism is about yanking a few souls into the lifeboats.

But look again at John 17:

> *My prayer is not for them alone. I pray also for those who will believe in me through their message, that all of them may be one, Father, just as you are in me and I am in you. May they also be in us so that the world may believe that you have sent me. I have given them the glory that you gave me, that they may be one as we are one—I in them and you in me—so that they may be brought to complete unity. Then the world will know that you sent me and have loved them even as you have loved me.*
>
> **JOHN 17:20–23**

There is a glorious love that flows from the Father to the Son and from the Son to his people. As we stand together in this Fountain—as we are united together in this love—'*then the world will know*'!

Remember how Jesus sent out his disciples to the nations:

> *Again Jesus said, 'Peace be with you! As the Father has sent me, I am sending you.' And with that he breathed on them and said 'Receive the Holy Spirit.'* **JOHN 20:21–22**

Again we see the initiative is from above. *Down* comes the Son of the Father to rescue the world that he loves. *Down* comes the Spirit of Christ to give us heaven's peace. And now, *out* to the nations we go.

Trinitarian evangelism is 'Down and Out'. The triune God doesn't need converts to be complete. He is not empty, needing to be filled. He is full and delights to share. Our mission flows from his fullness. Therefore trinitarian evangelism frees us from desperately 'gaining converts'. Instead we're all about 'offering Christ'.

I get that phrase from two 18th-century evangelists, John Wesley and George Whitfield. At the end of a hard day's evangelism—sometimes preaching to tens of thousands in the open air—they would reflect on what happened. They might sometimes speak of people being 'awakened to' the love of God, but they didn't talk in terms of 'decisions made'. Instead they rejoiced in the fact that the message had been delivered: 'I offered them Christ!' is what they would write in their journals, and then they slept! That seems a healthy way to be.

Think of all the things that Christians *do* in order to share their faith: running children's clubs and youth groups; inviting friends, family and neighbours to church;

organising evangelistic events and mission weeks; giving out books; sharing videos...

These are some great things to do. All of them can be done healthily. But beware: all of them can be done unhealthily too. The *way* we do any of these activities and the *why* is crucial. Let's say, for instance, you join a new club with the hope of being a witness. Sounds great (and it is) if it springs from 'Down and Out' motives. But if you're motivated by an 'Up and In' evangelism, you'll end up using the club and its members rather than serving them. You won't love them for *them*. You'll use them for what you can get out of them. And three things will probably happen: they'll notice, you'll get frustrated and it won't last.

Instead, consider Paul's 'Down and Out' model in 1 Thessalonians:

> *Because we loved you so much, we were delighted to share with you not only the gospel of God but our lives as well.*
> **1 THESSALONIANS 2:8**

Paul considers it a gift when he shares his life, and he considers it a gift when he shares the gospel. Both his service and his witnessing are offerings. So then, as we're swept up in the same Spirit-filled movement, we too can move beyond the comfortable and out into the world. In this 'Down and Out' flow we can volunteer at the homeless shelter, help out with the toddler group, start a book club, join a sports team, or just have the neighbours over. In all this you can love people well *and* offer them Christ. You can give your time to the Scouts *and* give them Jesus when the opportunities arise. Sharing life and sharing Christ are both gifts because, on the Down and Out model, everything flows from love, not need; from delight, not duty. Healthy evangelism springs from fullness.

As we live and love in this way, we'll look different. And chances are, our friends and family will notice.

SEED TO SCATTER 4:

THAT'S WHY I TRY TO LIVE DIFFERENTLY

Since the Jesus-God is so different, life with him will also be different. Not that we perfectly follow him—not even close. But in a world where everyone is chasing an 'Up and In' life, receiving from the 'Down and Out' God will have consequences. The way we see the world, the way we want to live, and our priorities will change. Our families will see us making time for church each Sunday. Our colleagues will see the way we forgive while others hold onto a grudge. Our friends will notice our approach to social media and money. Our neighbours will see us fostering or volunteering or welcoming new residents.

Flagging up those *practical* differences can be more effective than a dozen conversations about our *theological* differences. That's why it's important both to live differently and to be ready to describe *why*.

Of course it's best if your friend is the one who notices the difference! Then you just get to supply the reasons. And that's the heart of it. Can you connect these practical differences to your faith? Perhaps it will come out in phrases like…

- It might sound trite but I genuinely believe 'God is love' and that makes a difference when I think about how I'm going to live…
- I mean it's in the book: Jesus literally said 'It's better to give than receive', and I've definitely found that to be the case…
- I reckon the whole world is trying to grab at life to fill our emptiness and it's making us miserable. In the Bible God pours himself out and we get swept along. It's a different way to live…

You'll have to make it sound like you and you'll have to tailor it to the practicalities you're discussing, but try for yourself. Below, name three practical differences your faith makes in your life and then try to explain them as best you can in terms your friends might understand…

SPEND SOME TIME CONSIDERING YOUR OWN ANSWERS. YOU MAY WANT TO JOT DOWN SOME THOUGHTS HERE...

I try to live differently in *this* area…

Because…

I try to live differently in *this* area…

Because...

I try to live differently in *this* area...

Because...

'I COULD NEVER DO THAT'

I was known as 'Rev' in my cricket team back in Australia. This was long before I was ordained. I was actually a public servant at the time (in the UK I'd be called a civil servant). But I was as close to a clergyman as many in my team had met. We were on tour in Sri Lanka, enjoying a drink by the pool, and two teammates wanted to know why I was leaving Sydney to work for a London church. It seemed crazy to two guys working in finance. One of them in particular had set his sights on endless travel, early retirement and buying a yacht. He was making very good progress along that path.

'I'm far too selfish to do anything like that,' he said, referring to my upcoming move.

'Anything like what?' I asked.

'Do-gooding!' he said, knocking back the rest of his drink. As we laughed I tried to picture what they thought my life would look like in London: no doubt endless soup kitchens heaving with Cockney urchins asking for 'More'.

The conversation went many places from here. To begin with I tried to clarify what I'd be doing. Yes, a lot of menial service, and yes some charitable work with the homeless. But largely, I told him, I wanted to spend my time telling people about Jesus. I thought that would make him curious about why 'telling people about Jesus' was so important. No chance. He was set on the idea that 'Rev' was giving up a comfortable job to go and be a Do-Gooder. So I changed tack.

I stopped trying to distinguish between good works and the good news. Instead I decided to bring together good works and 'the good life'. So I said: 'Goodness is good, though, right?!' This struck my friends as a genuinely new thought. It became obvious in the conversation that my friends considered good works as one kind of thing (involving nuns and social workers) while 'the good life' is something very different (involving sports cars and Wall Street slime balls). There are do-gooders and there are those living the good life, and never the twain shall meet. *But what if goodness is actually, you know, good?*

This became a great conversation. Because at the heart of it, we were talking about ultimate reality. Is ultimate reality about grasping selfishly at life or is it about pouring yourself out in service? They thought the former (but they were glad for do-gooders who bucked the trend). I thought the latter. But I reckon you can have your cake and eat it. You can do good *and* live a good life—a fulfilling, meaningful, joy-filled life. Because ultimate reality *is* self-giving love. To live in line with that is to live with the grain of the universe. It's good. It's actually good to be good. And that's because of who God is.

As I'm often saying, 'Some people think the meaning of life is a very difficult subject. In the Bible it's simple: *Receive the love of God and pass it on*. That's the good life!' Far better than sports cars or yachts.

My friends weren't yet convinced but they had something to think about. And it came about not because of a gospel presentation or a conversational technique. It arose because of a life-choice that made no sense to them. The great challenge in evangelism is not so much to answer our friend's questions about the faith. The challenge is to live the kinds of lives that provoke them.

QUESTIONS FOR REFLECTION

- How does the truth of THREE connect to the primacy of love? How would you explain it to a friend who's not a Christian?
- What's the difference between 'Up and In' mission and 'Down and Out' mission?
- Thinking about the evangelistic activities you're involved with, are there ways they might have fallen into an 'Up and In' framework? What could you do about that?
- What practical differences does your faith make to your life? How would you explain those differences to friends in as simple and compelling way as you can?

321

THE WORLD'S TWO-NESS

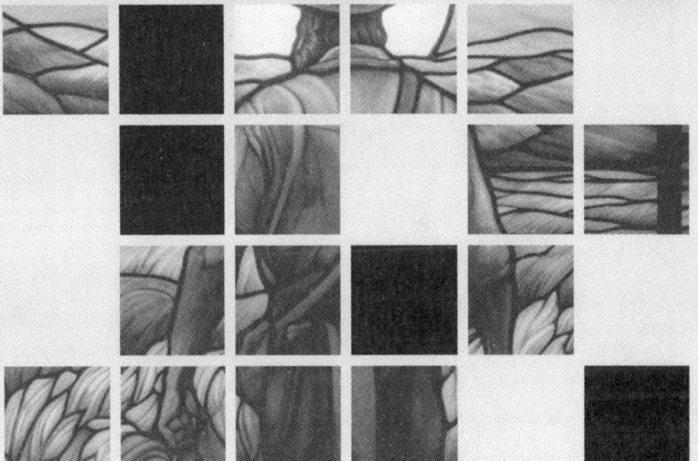

CHAPTER 5

FALLING DOWN

WHAT GETS YOU DOWN?

'FALLING DOWN' IS EPISODE 5 OF THE 321 COURSE.

WATCH IT NOW

Alternatively read chapter 5 of *How to See Life: A Guide in 321*

WHAT'S THE STORY?

Picture this: A spotlight shines from heaven and a voice calls out: 'Step into the light.' What part of you would want to? What part of you wouldn't?

There is a split-ness to us. On one hand, there's the person we should be, on the other is the person we are. This is what I'm calling the TWO-ness of humanity. One of the ways the Bible describes that TWO-ness is by speaking of Adam and Jesus. Jesus represents who we should be, Adam represents who we are—all of us.

Once I made a widower cry. It's not something I planned, nor is it a strategy I recommend, but I learnt something valuable in the process. Here's what happened. The man's wife had died just as they were approaching retirement. They were looking forward to trips and hobbies and endless time with the grandkids, but no longer. She was gone.

Everything changed for her husband who, unlike his wife, had never really considered spiritual things. In fact, it seemed to me that he'd never really considered *hard* things. And maybe those two facts were linked. He was the personification of 'stiff upper lip' and though I'd shared the gospel with him in different ways, nothing seemed to be getting through.

One day, though, after the funeral I checked in with him. Having prayed about it, I took a deep breath and asked one of those 'How are you *really*?' questions. This time I was determined not to be fobbed off. He gave it a good go: 'Oh it's just wonderful the way people have rallied around. The children have been a rock. And work could not be more supportive. I should think we've had *hundreds* of condolence cards…'

He kept going with the consolations for quite a while. I let him. After a pause I said a phrase that I wasn't exactly planning to say. It was very clunky and I wish I'd phrased it differently but out it tumbled: 'It's not enough though, is it?'

Hardly profound words. Maybe callous given the situation. But for some reason those six words got through. He cracked. He cried—the first time I'd seen him do it. As he got out his hanky, I continued, 'Oh James, it really, *really, REALLY* sucks. And all the condolence cards in the world don't really help, do they?' In between nose blows he squeaked out a little 'No'.

Here was an actual connection—something missing in all our prior interactions. And by the end of that conversation we were talking about Jesus in a profound and heartfelt way. We got to Jesus, but James was only able to receive when he'd laid down his self-sufficiency.

SEED TO SCATTER 5:

WHAT GETS YOU DOWN?

It could be disease, depression, decay, death or any number of broken aspects in the world—think about what grieves your heart most. Think about *why* it grieves you too. What good thing is being frustrated? What beauty is being marred? What hope is being dashed?

SPEND SOME TIME CONSIDERING YOUR OWN ANSWERS. YOU MAY WANT TO JOT DOWN SOME THOUGHTS HERE...

What gets me down...

____

____

____

____

____

Why? (What good thing is being thwarted? What hope is being dashed?)

____

____

____

____

Considering *What gets you down?* might seem odd in evangelism. After all, aren't we meant to be promoting God, not bemoaning his handiwork? But actually it's vital. When we name the fallenness of the world we are connecting with our friends, resonating with issues of the heart, telling the truth, and testifying to the fact *such things should not be*.

That's powerful because if we can all agree that such things *should not* be then we are agreed that there's a way the world *ought* to run. But why? Why should the world be any different to how it is now? An *ought* or a *should* seems like something that only makes sense with God—and specifically the kind of God who made things 'good' in the beginning and who promises a wonderful finale at the end.

When we ask our friends what gets them down, we are pressing into C.S. Lewis' 'crooked lines'.[3] In *Mere*

3 C.S. Lewis, *Mere Christianity* (Harper Collins, 2001), p. 38–39.

Christianity, Lewis describes how he moved from atheism to belief in God. It happened when he looked full in the face of this world's brokenness and called it Wrong—Wrong with a capital W. There came a point when he saw 'what gets us down' as more than ugly, painful or unfortunate. It was something Evil, something objectively Not Right. But of course if these things are Not Right then we're saying that there's something that *is* Right. Right with a capital R.

Lewis likened it to seeing crooked lines. You can only call them Crooked because you've got some understanding of Straight. If there's no such thing as Straight Lines then there's no such thing as Crooked Lines. Lines are just lines and the stuff that gets you down just happens.

But we know that what gets us down is capital-W Wrong and so, in photo negative, we are considering the truth that something Right stands above and beyond this world. Let's put it in the language of TWO. There is a way things *are*—represented by Adam. But it makes us cry out for the way things *should be*. In short, it makes us cry out for Jesus. That's why pressing into 'fallenness' can be so fruitful in evangelism.

And it's why, in our evangelism, admitting to our own Adam-like nature—our sin!—is so powerful.

WHAT ARE WE LIKE?

I'll often tell my friends what an idiot I am: 'No one has sabotaged my own success and happiness better than I have.

And if you get too close to me, I'll sabotage your success and happiness too. I'll say horrible things to the people I love and then say "I don't know what came over me". But nothing came over me, it all came out of me. What am I like?'

That last question isn't really rhetorical. Quite often people respond, 'Ah Glen, you're only human.' At which point you're in the middle of a profound conversation about human nature.

We are like Adam. That's how the Bible presents things. After all, the name 'Adam' just means 'Man'—i.e. 'Humanity'. In Genesis 2, Humanity is on top of the world. In Genesis 3, Humanity turns from God into mistrust and selfishness. We then read about Humanity driven from God's presence, estranged and downcast. We are Adam. *What he did we're always doing.*

Our friends and family recognise something of this instinctively. They are all living out the story of Genesis 3. First there's *suspicion* as Adam and Eve mistrust the overflowing bounty of God. Second there's *selfishness*, as they grasp at their own vision for life. Third, there's *slavery* as they turn to the forbidden fruit as their source of real life. Fourth, there's *self-justification* when they get exposed in their shameful folly. Fifth, there are *screw-ups*, as this ideal couple in an ideal situation still manage to ruin it all. And finally, there's *separation* when they are excluded from the presence of God. That's Adam and Eve. That's you and me. And that's your friends.

At this point, people sometimes object: 'Surely you don't believe "Adam and Eve" and all that?!' There are lots of responses to this (check out the FAQ section at the end of this book), but here's a quick one: 'Are you kidding? The Adam story is always happening. It's the happening-est story in the world! I bet it's been happening to you today!' If our friends are honest, they'll see it.

This is the fundamental point about our fallenness. It's not that humanity is as bad as bad can be—it isn't. But we have fallen from fellowship with God and, as regards restoring ourselves to our original heights, we are helpless—as helpless as helpless can be. We are suspicious of God, selfish for life on our own terms, enslaved to our foolish God-substitutes, self-justifying about our true nature, screwing up in baffling self-sabotage and separated from the life of God.

What's more, we can't undo our misdeeds. Fallenness is part of our story now. It's the way things are. We're all born outside the Garden, and the entrance is barred. We cannot unbake the cake. We cannot get the toothpaste back in the tube. We cannot save ourselves.

You don't have to mention the name 'Adam', and I'm certainly not expecting you to say to your friends, 'Let's turn in our Bibles to Genesis 3…' I'm simply wanting us all to think in these terms so that it flows from our lips. Here are some things I might say in conversation that allude to the truth of Adam:

- I feel like I'm my own person, then I open my mouth... *and out comes my father!*
- You try to escape your parents and then you become them.
- The older I get, the more I see that we are the product of our families—for better and for worse.
- We are family, right? Everyone in the human race—that's what the Bible says. It's just we're a dysfunctional family...
- The whole world is an extended family and we all share a family likeness. Some traits are good, some are terrible, but deep down we share the same human nature, wouldn't you say?

You'll notice that these statements describe two aspects of the Adam story: our sin and our solidarity. Both are important.

You might think the topic of sin is a drawback in evangelism. Isn't it unpopular to point out people's faults? Yes and no. No one likes being told that they're a sinner but in a culture that prizes authenticity, talking about our brokenness has a ring of truth to it. If we own up to our own fallenness, that sense of honesty connects with people. But secondly, the point about solidarity resonates too. We love the idea of community (our practice of it might be another matter, but we love the idea of it!). When we speak of our solidarity with one another it is both attractive and theologically necessary. It's necessary because the gospel is all about connection.

If we don't appreciate the connectedness of the human family we will never understand how Jesus can save. If human beings are just atomised individuals (which is certainly how most of my friends think), then nothing about the Jesus story makes sense. He might have become a human, lived, died and rose again, but what is that to *us*? How are *we* involved? We're just individuals, aren't we?

The Adam story says No. In fact, five minutes thought about the human condition says No. That's why I try to get people thinking about their family tree.

WHO DO YOU THINK YOU ARE?

The show was a surprise hit for BBC2, to the point where they switched it to primetime on BBC1. *Who Do You Think You Are?* found popularity by foregrounding the sort of thing your Aunty Kath does in her spare time: genealogies. Each episode would follow a celebrity as they investigated their family history, unearthing royal ancestors as well as family scandals along the way.

If I did the show I'd want to investigate Ann Forbes a little more. She's my great, great, great, great grandmother. In fact she's the English ancestor of about 6,000 Australians. That's because she was a convict who sailed on the First Fleet that landed in Botany Bay in 1788. Her crime was theft. She stole 10 yards of printed cotton from a London market and was sentenced to death. Eventually that was commuted to life transportation but I've often thought the day her life was saved from the hangman's noose was the day my life was saved too.

If I'm asked, nearly a quarter of a millennium later, why I'm alive, one answer is: a judge in Southwark had mercy. (Not a lot of mercy—but enough for my purposes!) If you ask, why I'm Australian, one answer is that someone committed a crime and was exiled. In fact that's true for all 6,000 descendants of Ann Forbes.

Your family tree will involve similar stories. At some point in your genealogy someone crossed an ocean, or left the monastery, or ran off with the chambermaid, and your family line veered off in a completely new direction. Your life is now profoundly different from what might have been because of decisions made centuries before your birth.

This isn't the modern way to think. Which is why the success of *Who Do You Think You Are?* was so surprising. We are constantly told today that we are the masters of our fate, the captains of our soul. We choose the course of our lives, it's all in our hands cos we're free, baby!

But when you watch a show like *Who Do You Think You Are?* you realise that our modern beliefs are ridiculous. I've had no choice whatsoever about where I was born, when, to whom, my upbringing, my genes, my predispositions to a thousand conditions and illnesses and psychological preferences. Those have shaped me at the deepest level.

My choices have shaped my life a little. As I got older, I began to be able to choose the clothes I wore and the music I listened to. Increasingly I chose the subjects I studied at school, then I chose when I left home, and where to, and the friends that I made, and the woman that I married. These are important choices. But so much of my identity was already baked in long before I decided anything. I never asked to be thrown into this world. Every one of my 20,000 genes 'came as standard' in the model of humanity I was gifted. The factory settings are unalterable. There are no updates and no upgrades.

The Adam story is a way of teaching us—and our friends—what every child of Adam should already know: we're all in the same boat. If that's true then it's a myth that we can strike out (like the younger brother in the prodigal son parable) and find freedom in independence. It's also a myth that we can pick up a shovel (like the older brother in the same story) and prove ourselves in independence. We *are* in this together. And we're in a mess.

THE WORLD IS SHAPED…

Importantly, Adam explains more than the human condition. He also explains the world. Remember that Adam is taken from the ground (his very name 'Adam' comes from the Hebrew word 'Adamah', meaning 'ground'). He's a dirtbag, kissed by heaven:

> *The LORD God formed a man [Adam] from the dust of the ground [Adamah] and breathed into his nostrils the breath of life, and the man became a living being.* **GENESIS 2:7**

The man who *is* earth is vitally connected to the earth. He is given dominion over it. The world turns on the God-Man axis. When all is well between God and man, all is well with the world. But when man falls, the earth is knocked off its axis, so to speak. Everything unravels. All hell breaks loose.

Every experience we have of the world's brokenness is an experience of a fall. We hate disease because it's a fall from physical health. We hate depression because it's a fall from mental health. We hate disorder and decay because it's a fall from order and beauty. We hate death because it's a fall from life.

Every time our friends see the brokenness of the world we are situating ourselves in the *second* Act of a drama. And Christians can say 'Of course! If life is a drama then we *are* in Act 2. We've come from Act 1—an original goodness—and we're heading for a happy ending. Act 3 is coming! But right now we're in the messy middle.'

Suddenly we're longing for the Second Adam.

QUESTIONS FOR REFLECTION

- What is attractive and compelling about the Adam story?
- What is difficult about it? How would you seek to address those difficulties with your friends? (Don't forget the FAQs.)
- How do you answer the question, *What gets you down?*

CHAPTER 6

UP!

THAT'S WHY I HAVE HOPE

'UP!' IS EPISODE 6 OF THE 321 COURSE.

WATCH IT NOW

Alternatively read chapter 6 of *How to See Life: A Guide in 321*

WHAT'S THE STORY?

Picture this: A man falls down a deep hole. Try as he might, he cannot climb out. Various passers-by yell down advice… or comfort… or rebuke. One man, though, dives in. He gets dirty. He gets hurt. But he hoists the man on his shoulders and lifts him out. This is the difference that Jesus makes. Other religions and philosophies are like the passers-by. They give advice to fallen people (or comfort or rebuke). But the gospel is not good advice, it's the good news that Christ has come down into our plight, suffered our curse and risen again. Christians are both realists and optimists. We're realistic enough to acknowledge the depths of our problems, and optimistic enough to hope for a glorious future.

'MY LIFE IS CURSED'

First she told me about her problems, then she told me about all the 'solutions' that had made things worse. And here she was: done in, tangled up and stressed out—unable to see a way through.

'My life is cursed,' she said, pausing to see if I'd disagree with her. To be fair, this is usually the cue to say, 'Don't be silly, I'm sure things will turn around. You deserve some luck'—that kind of thing. But I surprised her (and surprised myself a bit) by saying, 'Yeah, that's worth thinking about. Do you believe in curses?'

She did. She'd had experience of Spiritualism (this was the first I'd heard of her history with it) and she was definitely not an atheist. She believed in curses and she saw a spiritual dimension to her life. As a younger Christian I don't think I'd have pressed into that 'curse' language. But the more I've studied the Adam story, the more I've seen this way of thinking as fruitful.

We ended up talking about the world having a grain to it, and if you go against the grain you get splinters. That made sense to her. And I told her I believed that the grain of the universe is love. She agreed. But particularly, I said, it's the love of God. She had no problem with that. And so I talked about *how* the Bible can say God is love. It can say God is love because God is a Father always loving his Son, Jesus. We're made for that Father, but we're like runaway kids.

I asked if she knew the story of the prodigal son. She said she thought so, but I told it to her anyway (turns out she didn't know it). I talked through how we're all running away from the love we're made for and trying to get free in the far country. But the money always runs out and the famine always hits. We want independence, we end up alone. We aim for a feast and end up starving. We try to get free, we end up lost. That's life under the curse. Everything is frustrated because we're basically trying to get from the world everything we left behind with God.

I told her my own experiences of the curse—of the frustration of life 'far from God', and what a relief it is to come 'home'. It's not that life becomes easy. In some ways it's harder. But God is not on your back, he's on your side.

We ended up speaking of the deepest truths imaginable. And a conversation that began heavy ended with great hope. Speaking of judgement is necessary in evangelism. It can also be fruitful.

GOD OF LOVE / GOD OF JUDGEMENT

For five chapters we've pressed into the love of God. The God revealed by Jesus is a Father loving his Son in the joy of the Holy Spirit. God *is* love. When God created the world through his Word and Wisdom, Jesus, he was full of rejoicing. Notice the way Wisdom puts it in Proverbs 8:

> *I was constantly at [God's] side.*
> *I was filled with delight day after day,*
> *rejoicing always in his presence,*

rejoicing in his whole world
and delighting in the human race.

PROVERBS 8:30–31

In the beginning there was delight. The problems only came when sin entered the world. And even then, God's anger and curses follow *because* of his love. Anger is not the opposite of love. Indifference would be the opposite of love. If someone didn't care about the hideous evil of this world we would not call them loving. We would call them a sociopath. But our friends need to know: God cares infinitely. And one sign of his infinite care is his anger.

It's important when we're talking to people to explain that God's anger is different to our anger. His is righteous—ours is often self-righteous. God is not controlled by his anger—unlike us when we 'fly off into a rage'. God's anger is proportionate to the evil that provokes it whereas we regularly blow things out of proportion. God is love and remains love, even as he is angry at the things that damage, deny or destroy that love. But still he *is* angry. And that present tense is important.

Again and again the Bible speaks of God's anger in the present tense. He displays his anger every day (Psalm 7:11), he reveals it from heaven (Romans 1:18), and it remains on those who refuse his Son (John 3:36). Yes there is a future judgement where our status with God is confirmed, but there is also present judgement. As pastor and author Steve Levy says, right now there are 'trailers' for the 'feature film'.[4] There are experiences of 'hell on earth' that shout to us all: *'You do not want to go there!'* Lostness in this life is a screeching alarm to awaken us: *do not get lost forever.*

This means that some of the best depictions of God's judgement are not medieval paintings or Hollywood horror movies, they are experiences of disconnected living in the here and now. As our friends go through suffering they may say, 'I feel like I'm cursed.' And at times we need to take a deep breath to say, 'That's worth thinking about…'

But wonderfully, we don't have to stop there.

YOU MUST BE BORN AGAIN

Nicodemus was, perhaps, the most impressive man in Israel (John 3:1–21). He was wealthy, powerful, morally upright and, it seems, the chief Bible scholar of his day—'Israel's teacher' (John 3:10). But all of those are achievements of 'the flesh', our humanity in Adam. But, as Jesus says to Nicodemus, 'Flesh gives birth to flesh, but the Spirit gives birth to spirit' (John 3:6). Life in Adam only gives birth to more life in Adam. If we want a different kind of life—the life of the Spirit—then

4 Steve Levy, *John 3:36*, online audio recording, 10 March 2024, <http://www.mountpleasantchurch.org.uk/getfile.php?type=sermons&id=794.mp3> [accessed 23 April 2024].

we need to be 'born from above' which is another way of translating 'born again' (John 3:3). Heaven's life is received not earned.

> *No one has ever gone into heaven except the one who came from heaven—the Son of Man.* **JOHN 3:13**

Our natural lives are built like the Tower of Babel—up, up, up we strive. Some of our family and friends come across very impressive, like Nicodemus. Others less so. But everyone is naturally aiming in the wrong direction. The life of the flesh is cursed, it cannot reach the life of heaven. But the one from heaven comes down: the Son of Man.

Here Jesus is using his favourite name for himself. The name 'Son of Man' means he is the very essence of humanity. He is human nature embodied. If Adam is 'humanity', Jesus is the epitome of humanity. The real thing. Later in the New Testament Paul would pick up this idea of Jesus 'the Last Adam'—the answer to the first (cf. Romans 5:12–21; 1 Corinthians 15:20–49). This is the central truth of the TWO in 321:

> *The world is shaped by TWO representatives: Adam and Jesus.*

Here is incredible hope. Yes we are born into sin and curse and we can't update or upgrade. But with Jesus we genuinely see Humanity 2.0. Here is a life unstained by sin and curse—a blessed life in connection with God. And he comes down from heaven to freely give it to us.

The world is shaped by TWO representatives. Adam has taken us down into the perishing life of the flesh. This is the life we're born into. But Jesus has taken flesh as the Second Adam. He has *represented* us. In taking on our human condition and dying our death on the cross he has taken Adam's perishing life where it belongs—to curse and judgement. When he rose again, he brought humanity through the death we deserve and into a glorified resurrection life.

He's like a needle who has pierced the black shroud of death and come through to the other side. If we are connected to him, like thread to the needle, we will be pulled through to his kind of life forever.

> *For God so loved the world that he gave his one and only Son, that whoever believes in him shall not perish but have eternal life.* **JOHN 3:16**

Notice the TWO kinds of life described here. There is the kind of life that Adam has: 'perishing'. Then there is the kind of life that Christ has: 'eternal'. We're born into perishing life but Christ is given to us as God's gift. All who receive him by faith are born again into *his* life. We remain members of the human family but, incredibly and eternally, we join God's.

So then, think of yourself in Adam: before you had done anything, good or bad, your identity was settled—sinner!—and so was your inheritance—death! But now think of yourself in Christ: before you had done anything, good or bad, your identity is settled—child!—and so is your inheritance—eternal life! How? Only through Jesus, the Second Adam. My neighbour felt so cursed, but here is Christ's offer: be free; be blessed; be born again!

As the Second Adam, Jesus has taken up our humanity and passed it through the furnace of the cross and into the glory of his resurrection. To see him on the cross is to see him lifting our humanity up to the purging flames of judgement. But to see him on the third day is to see 'Man' where 'Man' belongs, on the far side of death and curse, no longer perishing but radiant with immortal glory. There is a way through judgement and into eternal life—the way is Jesus himself. And if we fix our eyes on him we have an unparalleled hope.

HOPE FOR THE WORLD?

From the perspective of a non-Christian, what is the most striking thing about a Christian? What will provoke the most curiosity from an unbelieving world? What will cause the people we know to sit up and take notice?

In John 13:34–35 Jesus points to 'love'. In particular, the love of brothers and sisters in the church family. That is the most fundamental Christian distinctive and in chapter 8 we'll press into that. But alongside love, Peter gives another distinctive: hope. In the Bible's most famous verse about personal evangelism, Peter urges us to 'be prepared' for questions about our hope. It's not just love that will set us apart. Hope will really stand out in a hopeless world:

> *But in your hearts revere Christ as Lord. Always be prepared to give an answer to everyone who asks you to give the reason for the hope that you have. But do this with gentleness and respect…* **1 PETER 3:15**

Adam's world is not a hopeful place. We all know how it goes: we raise ourselves up and then tumble down. The way of Adam is fundamentally tragic. We may enjoy a brief moment in the sun, but the end is darkness. It's life and then death. But there is a group of people on planet earth who inhabit a different story. As regards the flesh—as regards biological reality—we are perishing. But in Jesus—the Second Adam—we have a God who joins himself to humanity, and to the physical world, in order to raise us up. Jesus rose from the tomb and now, by the *Spirit* of Jesus, we don't go from life to death, we go from death to life. There's a happily ever after. A comedy not a tragedy.

This is different. As we saw in chapter 3, the world has no hope apart from Jesus. There's only one worldview that sees an eternal future for our bodies and our world.

Christianity is unique because it holds to this truth that the world is shaped by TWO representatives, Adam and Jesus and the TWO are not equals. Jesus is stronger than Adam. The Spirit is mightier than the flesh.

I'm always telling people how the Gospels end (see Luke 24 and John 20–21 especially). I describe what it was like when Jesus rose because, if he is 'the Son of Man', then he is revealing the future for humanity—the future of the world. And what does it look like beyond death? Long country walks with his friends, conversations long into the night about the stuff that really matters, fishing with mates, barbecues on the beach, tear-filled reunions, *lots* of good food together and coming face-to-face with the battle-scarred Lover of your soul. That's the life! That's eternal life according to Jesus.

In light of such an unparalleled happily ever after, Christians live with hope. And Peter reckons it's the kind of hope that, at times, our non-Christian friends will notice. They will ask us to give reasons for the hope we evidently have. Let's be prepared then.

SEED TO SCATTER 6:

THAT'S WHY I HAVE HOPE

The context for this seed will almost certainly be an admission that 'things look bleak right now.' Your opportunity to say something will probably come in the midst of discussions about hopelessness. But, against that backdrop, the hope that you have shines brighter.

SPEND SOME TIME CONSIDERING YOUR OWN ANSWERS. YOU MAY WANT TO JOT DOWN SOME THOUGHTS HERE...

The hope that I have…

The reasons I have hope…

The difference hope makes to me…

FROM CURSE TO HOPE

I told you about my neighbour who felt cursed. I didn't tell you how the conversation ended. At some point we got onto the subject of hope. It's something we cannot live without. And if we feel the curse, we cry out for it all the more. I told my friend a story originally by John Newton, the slave trader turned preacher and the author of 'Amazing Grace'.[5]

He said that, for a Christian, life is like a journey to a solicitor's office in London where you're about to receive an inheritance of millions. Imagine it. But on the way, the carriage breaks down and you have to walk the last mile on foot. And maybe you step in horse poo. And your hat blows away. And it starts to rain. But you're about to become a millionaire.

Christians still deal with the curse of Adam's world (the horse dung, the wind and the rain). And we're still caught up in the selfishness of Adam's flesh. But we have Christ's Spirit—a deposit guaranteeing a gargantuan inheritance. And that makes all the difference. Without that hope, the curses of Adam's world are intolerable. *With* that hope, you can even find yourself skipping through the storm!

---

5 Quoted in Richard Cecil, 'Memoirs of the Rev. John Newton', in *The Works of the Rev. John Newton Volume 1* (Banner of Truth, 1985), p. 107.

As we finished, I offered to pray for her and she said 'Yes please.' God is still at work in her in amazing ways but it started by taking the two Adams seriously.

QUESTIONS FOR REFLECTION

- What important elements of the gospel would we lose if we ditched the two Adams?
- In what ways are sin, curse and judgement difficult to talk about in evangelism? In what ways might they be engaging and fruitful?
- How can you speak of Christian hope in ways that will make sense to your friends?

321

YOUR ONE-NESS

CHAPTER 7

CHAMPION

WHAT GETS YOU THROUGH?

'CHAMPION' IS EPISODE 7 OF THE 321 COURSE.

WATCH IT NOW

Alternatively read chapter 7 of *How to See Life: A Guide in 321*

WHAT'S THE STORY?

Picture this: A South American footballer joins a Premier League team on the brink of relegation. Somehow he plays a miracle season, lifting the team out of danger and taking them all the way to Wembley where he singlehandedly wins them the FA Cup. His victory is the team's victory. One man wins. Millions celebrate.

This is just like the work of Christ, our Champion. As the Second Adam he takes responsibility for Team Humanity, shoulders our burdens, defeats our enemies, and shares his victory with us.

DO NOT TRY TO CONVERT ME

As we arranged to meet up the next day, Sam's late night message came through, caps-locked:

DO NOT TRY TO CONVERT ME
TO CHRISTIANITY!

We've known each other for nearly 30 years, since school. For the last 20-plus years I've been a Christian, something he's been fine about, as long as I keep it to myself. He is, as you can tell, *not* open to an evangelistic encounter! So what did we talk about the following day? Actually we spoke of the very deepest truths about God, his judgement and his grace. How come? Did Sam change his mind? Did I blunder through his boundaries and force an intervention? No and no. The truth is, God is good, prayer is powerful and *everything is ultimately about Jesus.*

The day after the email, I met my friend on a beach on the south coast. We had bacon sandwiches and flat whites and caught up on each other's news. We'd both had another child since last we met—ours by adoption.

'We've been thinking about adoption,' Sam said, 'how has it been?'

I told him about the hurdles, the screening process, the bureaucracy, the crying need, the appalling trauma faced by so many little ones. Then we spoke of the unique challenges adoption brings. Our own parents are across various oceans, so the support of church family has been crucial. But I brought it back to this: *'You've got to believe that unconditional love is really how people change and flourish—you've got to believe it down to your toenails.'*

Sam said he thought he did believe that. I told him it would be tested sorely and constantly, and that offering unconditional love like this will, at times, feel excruciating. But the alternative is hell—the hell of disconnection, of further distance, mistrust, fear and anger. The only answer is absorbing that hell and—somehow!—answering with grace. It feels excruciating—like getting crucified—but it's the only way.

'And look,' I said, 'I know you told me not to try to convert you but I'm not trying to convert you, I'm telling you what I need to hear for my *own* sanity. For Emma and me, it's genuinely our faith that sees us through. We really believe that absorbing the hell and paying back with love is how the universe operates—it's what God did. And now, with him, we get to see it at work in our little family. And it *does*. You know?'

And he really did seem to know. It was the deepest connection we've had concerning faith. Who knows where it will lead but that morning, in spite of his forewarnings, we ended up having a God conversation full of 'What gets you thinking?', 'What gets you up?', 'What gets you down?' and 'What gets you through?'

I learn two things from this: prayer is powerful and evangelism is pastoral.

PRAYER IS POWERFUL

I'd been praying for Sam for decades, and I prayed extra hard for this conversation. Lo and behold, a door was opened. Paul often uses this type of language in the New

Testament. He says 'a great door for effective work has opened to me' (1 Corinthians 16:9), or 'I went to Troas to preach the gospel of Christ and found that the Lord had opened a door for me' (2 Corinthians 2:12).

Do you ever feel like someone has—figuratively and spiritually—slammed the door shut on the gospel and double bolted it? Paul knows a way to pick the lock. See how prayer and the opening of doors go together in Colossians:

> *Devote yourselves to prayer, being watchful and thankful. And pray for us, too, that God may open a door for our message, so that we may proclaim the mystery of Christ, for which I am in chains. Pray that I may proclaim it clearly, as I should. Be wise in the way you act toward outsiders; make the most of every opportunity. Let your conversation be always full of grace, seasoned with salt, so that you may know how to answer everyone.* **COLOSSIANS 4:2–6**

Prayer wraps around every aspect of evangelism here. We pray for the capital-E Evangelists like Paul who have particular roles, gifting and open doors of opportunity. But prayer also precedes our own everyday evangelism. As we pray, we're helped to be wise, gracious and salty in our talk—providing some bite and savour to our faith conversations. And through our prayers it's not just doors that can be opened, it's hearts too.

In Philippi, Lydia heard the preaching of Paul and you might think the Apostle's powers of persuasion were the deepest cause of her conversion. But Acts 16:14 reminds us how faith really happens: 'The Lord opened her heart to respond to Paul's message.' Conversion is God's work. Since this is true, it would be foolish to spend all our time talking to our friends about God when, all the more, we should be talking to God about our friends! Our Father is the one who opens doors and hearts. And he opens our mouths too.

It's fascinating that perhaps the two greatest communicators in the Bible—perhaps in human history—pray for an open mouth. Neither David nor Paul rely on their natural abilities. In Psalm 51, David cries to the Lord:

Restore to me the joy of your salvation
and grant me a willing spirit, to sustain me.
Then I will teach transgressors your ways,
so that sinners will turn back to you.
Deliver me from the guilt of bloodshed, O God,
you who are God my Saviour,
and my tongue will sing of your righteousness.
Open my lips, Lord,
and my mouth will declare your praise.

PSALM 51:12–15

Here is a desperate plea to be forgiven, restored and recommissioned as a witness to the world. But David has confidence that his prayer would be answered—sinners would turn back to God through his words. If only God would open his mouth, David would declare soul-converting praise. And so he prays fervently.

Paul is also desperate for an open mouth in the New Testament:

> *Pray also for me, that whenever I speak, words may be given me so that I will fearlessly make known the mystery of the gospel…* **EPHESIANS 6:19**

Paul craves divine help and so he covets the prayers of the Ephesians. But if this is the desperation of Paul and David to plead for an 'open mouth' how much more should we do the same.

These are the prayers we pray for our own evangelism. It's also how we should pray for those with God-given platforms, pulpits and opportunities: open doors of opportunity; open hearts to receive the gospel; and open mouths to proclaim clearly and boldly.

Those kinds of prayers were definitely going on in the background to my conversation with Sam. But let's also consider another factor at play.

PASTORAL EVANGELISM

Picture someone who is *really* evangelistic. Usually people imagine a motor-mouth with the enthusiasm of a Labrador pup, the skin of a rhinoceros's hide, the social skills of a boisterous toddler and the patter of a telesales marketeer.

But what if I asked you to picture someone who is really *pastoral*? Now the image changes. It's endless cups of tea, frowns of concern, and a head cocked permanently to a 45 degree angle. We seem to live with a huge divide in our thinking between the evangelistic and the pastoral. I used to share this divided understanding. But then I met Henry Olonga.

Henry is a former international cricketer, a professional singer, a two-time TV talent show contestant (and one-time winner!), and a shining light for Jesus. He's famous for wearing a black arm-band during the 2003 Cricket World Cup to protest the death of democracy at the hands of Robert Mugabe. He had to flee for his life and has been in exile from his homeland ever since. I got to meet him about 10 years ago and he transformed the way I thought about evangelism.

I too was a cricketer and a Christian (though much shabbier at both), and I too wanted to shine for Jesus in my cricket club. But, looking back, I think my approach was all wrong. I thought that the best witness for Jesus would be someone who took five wickets, scored 100 runs, stayed late in the bar afterwards telling amazing mother-in-law gags *and* was a Christian. It was the attempt to be impressive *for Jesus* (ostensibly!). But Henry changed my outlook.

He would speak of Jesus in his team and he lived out his faith too. Motivated by Scripture, he made his stands against injustice when they weren't popular. I asked Henry if he found it fruitful to share his faith. And he said yes, but never in the ways he expected. Mostly his teammates did not want to know about spiritual things. Until, that is, life took a 'left turn'. If they got injured, or dropped from the team, or their girlfriend dumped them, *then* they were ready to hear. And that was when they sought out Henry for counsel.

After talking with Henry, I realised how wrong my approach had been. Who would a teammate want to confide in when life gets hard? Not the star or the joker—but the one with quiet integrity and wisdom. I realised that the goal is not to be the person everyone likes, but the person your friends turn to in times of need. Be the gently glowing lamp in the corner. When things get dark, people will gravitate towards you.

We often think of evangelism and pastoral care as very different undertakings. But in the Bible they are much closer. In Acts 20 for instance, we hear of evangelism as telling 'the good news of God's grace' (v24) while a pastor is a shepherd who defends the flock from 'savage wolves' (v29). Biblically speaking, evangelists are tenderer and pastors are tougher than our modern stereotypes. That's because evangelising and pastoring are much more similar than we think. Really it's the audience that's different, rather than the message or the tone. Here's the way I like to say it:

> *Pastoral care is evangelising Christians.*
> *Evangelism is pastoring non-Christians.*

The first half of this is important: Christians need to be evangelised too. Constantly. We grow in our walk with Jesus as we hear his good news again and again. But then we should grasp the second half: non-Christians need to be pastored. Our friends are perishing in Adam, walking through the valley of the shadow of death (Psalm 23:4). They are subject to the prince of this world who only comes to steal, kill and destroy (John 10:10). They desperately need a Good Shepherd—one to see them through the dark valley and into life in all its fullness (John 10:10–11). We have the privilege of pointing them to the only one who can pastor them through. Our evangelism is pastoral.

SEED TO SCATTER 7:
WHAT GETS YOU THROUGH?

Everyone must walk through 'the valley of the shadow of death', but who or what is shepherding us through? Our colleagues and friends are looking to inadequate or counterfeit shepherds and, as we pastor them, we can explore that by sowing this seed. When they tell us about the stress of debt or a bullying boss or caring for elderly parents, we can ask them what they're relying on. What keeps them going? When they tell us of battles with health or addictions or loneliness, what gets them through? And we can point them to the only *Good* Shepherd—the One who has pastored us.

SPEND SOME TIME CONSIDERING YOUR OWN ANSWERS. YOU MAY WANT TO JOT DOWN SOME THOUGHTS HERE...

What do you think your friends would say gets them through?

____

____

____

____

How has Jesus got you through the difficult times in life?

____

____

____

____

In my own evangelism the sentence that speaks most powerfully to friends (especially if they really know me) is, 'I couldn't have got through that without Jesus.' To my mind this is the very essence of our testimony to the world.

Testimonies are often considered the heart and soul of personal evangelism so you might be surprised to see how long it's taken for me to discuss them. I love testimonies. But if you ask me, a testimony is not, most basically, a description of how you became a Christian. And it's definitely not a grand drama in which you are the star, making your way from darkness into light. I've heard far too many testimonies like this, perhaps you have too. In some testimonies the darkness is a pit of immorality, in others it's a nighttime of intellectual doubts, but somehow the Christian is the Hero and the story gets wrapped up in a neat bow at the end.

There's another problem with considering testimonies like this. It puts huge pressure on those from Christian homes to completely fabricate 'wilderness wanderings' that were, in reality, a three-day city break to Babylon. When the standard model for the testimony is a darkness-to-light story, it's all too easy for Christians to crank up the contrast, completely downplaying the gospel light they received from their family and church, and foregrounding their dark nights of debauchery and doubt. But we don't have to play those games, because a Christian testimony is not our journey from darkness to light. Our Christian story is Christ's journey down into our darkness. So we can frame our testimonies with 'I couldn't have got through X without Jesus.'

What is X for you? In my evangelism, I might speak about the stresses of adoption, or a dozen other struggles. For you it could be bereavement or health issues or a relationship breakdown or redundancy or any time where Jesus met you in your darkness.

Perhaps this prompts you to tell the story of your conversion, which is great. But it might also prompt you to tell the story of how Jesus is carrying you right now, 60 years on. That is a wonderful testimony!

In *this* kind of story, we can never be the Hero. But Jesus most certainly is.

QUESTIONS FOR REFLECTION

- How are you tempted to neglect or sideline prayer when it comes to evangelism? What can you do to be more prayerful in your evangelism?
- Why do you think pastoral care and evangelism are often thought of as completely separate things? How have you seen (or how might you see) 'pastoral evangelism' working?
- As you consider the ways Jesus has got you through, how might you explain that in ways that connect with your friends?

CHAPTER 8

LOVE STORY

THAT'S WHAT I LOVE ABOUT MY CHURCH

'LOVE STORY' IS EPISODE 8 OF THE 321 COURSE.

WATCH IT NOW

Alternatively read chapter 8 of *How to See Life: A Guide in 321*

WHAT'S THE STORY?

Picture this: A prince marries a pauper. She is ashamed and in debt. He is royal and rich. And what happens when they marry? All his riches go to her and all her debts go to him. The moment they unite in marriage she has his name, his royalty, his family, his inheritance.

The church is the bride of Christ and together we enjoy an extraordinary ONE-ness. Not only are we ONE with Jesus, we are also brought into ONE-ness with his other brothers and sisters in the church. *Together* we know God's love and *together* we share it with the world.

WHAT IS A CHRISTIAN?

If you ask your friends, 'What is a Christian?' you might get some depressing answers. The other day I got, 'Someone who doesn't swear or smoke.' Once I got, 'Someone who thinks they're better than other people.' Ouch! Other common answers include 'Someone who goes to church', 'Someone who's born in a Christian country', or if they lived through the 80s, 'Someone who likes Cliff Richard and quiche.'

If we ask the New Testament the same question, we get one answer more than any other. Over 150 times it describes a Christian as someone who is 'in Christ'. The depth of our connection to Jesus is truly extraordinary. So extraordinary, we usually trade it for something a little more tame.

There is an 'under Christ' gospel:

We failed to submit to God in the beginning but we've realised our error. A Christian is someone who has chosen to bow to Jesus, our King.

There is a 'behind Christ' gospel:

He is our Rabbi, we are his disciples, learning the way of Jesus, following in his footsteps. A Christian is someone who's trying to be like Jesus, our Example.

There is a 'with Christ' gospel:

We have invited Jesus into our lives and now we go into the world with his divine presence and empowering. A Christian is someone who keeps close to Jesus, our Friend.

There is a 'through Christ' gospel:

> *Jesus is the means by which we can enter heaven. A Christian is someone who has taken advantage of Jesus, our Bridge.*

There is truth to all of these. Jesus *is* our King, Example, Friend and Bridge. But none of this represents the pinnacle of what is offered in the gospel. The greatest gift that Jesus offers us is Jesus! And this wonderfully simplifies our evangelism. I am like the football fan whose champion scores the winner. He does all the work but I share in his victory. I am like the pauper married to the prince and therefore united to him. All my debts go to him and all his riches come to me. I am like the passenger who's boarded a flight. I don't take off and fly to the destination, the plane does. I'm just 'in' it—now what happens to the plane happens to me.

I'm always using these illustrations in my evangelism. I find that people instantly get the grace of Jesus when I explain ONE-ness and it's the central truth of the ONE in 321:

> *You are born ONE with Adam. Be ONE with Jesus.*

To be in Christ is to know the most astonishing intimacy. You cannot get closer than in! 'Union with Christ' is the theological term for this truth. It works like this: through our first birth we are united to Adam by the flesh. Through our new birth we are united to Christ by the Spirit. Now we are children in the Son, anointed ones in the Anointed One, blessed in the Blessed One. And what a difference this makes in our evangelism.

Remember how Jesus calls himself the Light of the World (John 8:12). Stunningly he turns to his people—those who are ONE with him—and he tells them:

> *You are the light of the world.* **MATTHEW 5:14**

What Jesus is individually and by nature, we become corporately and by grace. And what does that mean for our witness to the world? He goes on:

> *A town built on a hill cannot be hidden. Neither do people light a lamp and put it under a bowl. Instead they put it on its stand, and it gives light to everyone in the house. In the same way, let your light shine before others, that they may see your good deeds and glorify your Father in heaven.* **MATTHEW 5:14–16**

Jesus doesn't say we *ought* to be the light. He doesn't tell us to shine a bit brighter. He never asks us to 'get on fire' for him. It's far deeper than that. We *are* the light of the world and so we shine. We can't *not* shine.

Notice what this means for evangelism. We can stop trying to crank up our brightness and instead own our true identity—we can simply remove the bowls obscuring and hiding our glowing lamps.

Perhaps think of the ways you hide your light 'under a bushel' (as the old King James translation put it). In what situations do you cover over your Christian identity? How do you shrink back instead of shining out? Pray about those tendencies and patterns. Jesus is teaching us here that if we could only put away our bowls and unashamedly *be* the Christians we are, then our light would shine before the whole world.

So we need to grasp our ONE-ness with Christ: we *are* the light of the world. But here's something else we need to grasp: our ONE-ness with each other. You see *we* are the light of the world. It's about our life *together.*

LOVE ONE ANOTHER

Have you ever noticed how few biblical verses tell you, directly, to share your faith? There are endless verses about sharing your stuff, giving money, forgiving people, loving your brothers and sisters and so on. But where are the verses that explicitly tell you—little old you—to get busy evangelising?

Even the most popular go-to verse on personal witness, 1 Peter 3:15 (which we looked at in chapter 6), talks about responding to our friends' questions rather than initiating a conversation. What's going on?

Essentially it's all about our ONE-ness. Christ's mission to the nations is not to send a million 'lone rangers' into enemy territory. Christ's mission is the church. And we go as ONE. When you read the Bible from this perspective you see that the whole thing is evangelistic, but it's evangelistic by being profoundly church-focused:

> *Jesus said… 'A new command I give you: love one another. As I have loved you, so you must love one another. By this everyone will know that you are my disciples, if you love one another.'* **JOHN 13:31, 34—35**

From the Father to the Son there is an eternal love crashing down like an almighty Niagara Falls. United to the Son we stand in that flow of love, filled by the Spirit. But we're not simply recipients. The Christian is not a reservoir collecting the love; we are a river, passing on this love to one another. As the church lives in—and lives *out*—this love, the world will take notice. Here's what they'll see:

> *No one has ever seen God; but if we love one another, God lives in us and his love is made complete in us.* **1 JOHN 4:12**

Here is an answer to the hiddenness of God. Do your friends ever complain to you, 'Where is God? I can't see him or sense him. If he's there, he seems completely hidden.' Actually the Bible gives two answers to this problem. Back in chapter 3 we considered the first answer. In John 1:18, we read that familiar phrase, 'No one has ever seen God'. In *that* verse God's invisibility is answered by Christ. The invisible God is made known in his 'one and only Son'. But in 1 John 4, we read that exact phrase again. In verse 12 we are also told that 'No one has ever seen God', but what is the answer this time? 'Love one another'!

God is made known in the world in two main ways: 1) The person of Christ; 2) The love of his people. What reveals God? Jesus and the church.

The loving union of church is incredibly powerful. It reveals something of God who is also a loving union. Therefore fruitful evangelism will serve and commend the church wherever it can.

SUPERNATURAL EVANGELISM

Part of my job involves driving around and speaking. This means I get through a lot of cars. I've been the fourth, fifth, sixth and seventh owner of a car, but I've always been the last owner. A few years ago I was on a motorway one Sunday evening when the cambelt went causing instant engine failure. I went from 70 miles an hour to zero in about five seconds. Thankfully I was able to get off the road onto the hard shoulder. I was eventually towed back. My car was left at a local garage and I came home, near midnight. On the doormat lay a complete surprise: an envelope with our church's logo on it but otherwise unmarked. I opened it to find £400 in cash. I still don't know who gave it to us. We hadn't told anyone about the breakdown.

The next morning I phoned up the garage to ask if they'd taken a look at my car and if so, how much is a fix. 'I'm afraid you're not going to like it,' said the mechanic. I knew what he was going to say next, I just knew it. It felt like I was in a play and we were all just reciting lines from a script. 'It'll be £400.'

I had goosebumps, amazed at the miracle. But I've become convinced that, in that moment, I was amazed at the wrong miracle.

'Let me tell you a funny story…' I said to the mechanic, telling him about the envelope with our church logo on and the £400 inside. He paused and asked, 'Someone from your church gave you £400 *anonymously*?!'

I'd been putting all the emphasis on the *400*—as though the greatest miracle is that God made the numbers match. God *did* make the numbers match but the more amazing thing was the sacrificial love. That's what the mechanic took from it all.

'What's the name of that church? I might go.' He was joking, but not completely. The thing that arrested his attention was a miracle, but it was the miracle of church life.

COMMENDING THE CHURCH (WITHOUT CONCEALING ITS FAULTS)

I am constantly speaking of my church in evangelism. I marvel at the different generations united together, different nationalities, cultures and classes all getting along; our care for one another; our ministries serving the community; the wealth of wisdom and experience to be called on; the fact that every week we confess our sins out loud together; the fact we take time out every week to reset, hear truth from the world's all-time bestseller, pray and sing together—awesome! Most of all I speak of the fact that we call ourselves 'church family' and we actually *are* family—brothers and sisters through thick and thin. 'By this all people will know…' Absolutely!

Now I recognise that some experiences of church are negative—some diabolical. I'm well aware of the stain of church abuse. It stinks to high heaven. Genuinely. If there has been sin and corruption, I am not for a moment advocating we whitewash the church's reputation. Jesus takes the opposite approach in Matthew 23, calling out the whitewash and revealing the uncleanness beneath. But the reason why church abuse is so wicked is because church is meant to be so good. It is meant to be a safe haven, a refuge, a hospital for sick sinners. In many places it *is* that. But not always.

Sometimes Matthew 23 is the Scripture to foreground: hypocrisy must be called out and evil must be revealed. But hopefully, in far more cases, we can point to a people who 'love one another'. And this is powerful. Commending the church is so important in evangelism because when we call people to Christ, we are also calling them to his body, the church. No one can have a church-less Christ any more than they can have a body-less head.

I say this because there are times we're tempted to throw the church under the bus. When we hear critiques of Christianity we might say: 'Ah, that's just church-ianity. Don't look at the church, look at Christ.' Occasionally there's a time and a place for that kind of comment. But never forget that Jesus stands there proudly pointing to his church. We should not be individuals proclaiming a 'Me and Jesus' gospel. We are members of the body and our life together witnesses to our Lord. We evangelise *with* church and *as* church.

SEED TO SCATTER 8:

THAT'S WHAT I LOVE ABOUT MY CHURCH

What about you? How would you talk about your church to your friends? You might well emphasise different aspects of church life with different people. And you'll often speak of the blessings of Christ's body in contrast to the curses of Adam's world. When talking to my friends I find myself commending church in response to the troubles we're discussing...

- Modern life is so segmented. It's fantastic at church to have people from so many cultures, generations and outlooks...
- Raising kids today is hard but I love my church family because we help each other out...
- Christians talk about our 'church family' a lot and it might sound a bit weird but it's really not. We actually function like a family. For instance, the other day...
- I love that every Sunday I go to a place where we all admit we've messed up, and we just get honest with each other and with God. Where else...

SPEND SOME TIME CONSIDERING YOUR OWN ANSWERS. YOU MAY WANT TO JOT DOWN SOME THOUGHTS HERE...

Here's what I love about my church:

____

____

____

____

HOW TO REACH THE WORLD

It was the last night of a university mission and Phil told me he was terrified of the gospel being true because if it was he couldn't imagine how he could justify anything other than a life of unceasing evangelism from that day on.

'If I became a Christian, I would have to spend every waking moment trying to save others,' he reasoned.

If life is short, hell is hot and eternity is long, the only informed and loving response would involve becoming a 24/7 warning siren blasted from the town square. There were two things that Phil had become convinced of: 1) Non-stop, indiscriminate witnessing is the only legitimate response to Christ; and 2) He's not that kind of guy.

I'm guessing many Christians agree and so make an uneasy peace by settling for a second- (or third-) class Christianity, leaving the *real* Christian life to those activists who can manage the non-stop evangelism thing.

What do we say to this? Well I asked Phil what he made of the New Testament he'd been reading. 'Do you see much of that kind of frenzied activism in the Bible?'

'Well,' he said, 'Paul was certainly an activist.'

'That's true,' I replied. 'But in his letters he has many opportunities to command that particular lifestyle for others. And what is the kind of life he commends?'

We agreed that 1 Thessalonians 4:11–12 summarised it well:

> *... make it your ambition to lead a quiet life: you should mind your own business and work with your hands, just as we told you, so that your daily life may win the respect of outsiders and so that you will not be dependent on anybody.*

At that point Phil asked me about where reaching the world fits in. As part of a long conversation I suggested to him that God's way of reaching the world has always been through the church. In fact, biblically speaking, world-reaching and church-building are ultimately the same thing. The church is a living organism—a body, a vine—and healthy organisms grow. Christ gives us his Spirit to unite us into one body, the church. And by the Spirit this body is built up: in love for Christ; in mutual love for each other; in maturity; in words of witness; in works of service; and, yes, in numbers. But *the church* is God's evangelistic strategy.

I asked him if this was a mission he could get on board with? There was tangible relief in his voice when he said 'Yes.' Within days he'd become a Christian and now, years later, his gifts are indeed being used by God to build up the church.

If we want to reach the lost, we should build the church. That's what Jesus said:

> *I will build my church, and the gates of Hades will not overcome it.* **MATTHEW 16:18**

Here Jesus promises a world-conquering kingdom. Gates do not advance—the church advances. Jesus is inverting the image we usually bring to mind when we consider the church's place in the world. We worry that the powers of darkness are besieging an embattled church. But no, it's the other way around. The church, built by Jesus, is on the move. It's his kingdom that will grow, plundering Satan's kingdom and bringing light where there was darkness.

So this is Jesus' strategy for world domination: grow the church. We are to nurture a community of love founded on the confession that Jesus is 'the Messiah, the Son of the living God' (Matthew 16:16). For 2,000 years, this remarkable mission has been progressively fulfilled and his wisdom utterly vindicated. If you want to reach the world, build the church. Together we fulfil Christ's commission. Yes, we might play different roles (more on that in the FAQs) but we're all involved in a global mission, even as we do the most grounded, local, practical thing imaginable: love one another.

QUESTIONS FOR REFLECTION

- In our thinking, how do we often divorce 'reaching the world' from 'building the church'? How can we unite them?
- What do you love about your church? How might you enthuse about it to friends in a way that connects?
- What are the particular gifts God has given you and how might they integrate with others in your church for evangelism?

321

A FINAL WORD ABOUT WORDS

A farmer went out to sow his seed. **MATTHEW 13:3**

When it comes to evangelism, this parable is endlessly encouraging. It prepares us so well for the realities of speaking life. Most soil types involve major barriers and complications. Therefore, what does evangelism feel like? *Hit and miss—mainly miss!* Wonderfully, though, Jesus gives us a view of the long run. In the end, what are the prospects for Jesus' kingdom? *World domination!*

This is our situation as we seek to share Jesus. We are surrounded by people who are wildly different in their receptivity to the gospel. But Jesus does not counsel us to give up hope. Nor does he complicate things with an elaborate mission strategy. The church has one job: sow the seed. In other words: *share the Word.* Speak life, you might say.

And perhaps we object and say, *But there's satanic opposition* (the first soil type). Jesus says, *I know. Sow the seed.*

We complain, *But people are so flaky, they don't stick with Jesus* (the second soil type). Jesus says, *I know. Sow the seed.*

We lament, *But the whole world is spiritually dominated, caught up with worry and wealth and everything other than God* (the third soil type). Jesus says, *I know. Sow the seed.*

There is no plan B. There is only plan A: sharing the word of Jesus. Even when weeds are sown in the field by an enemy (Matthew 13:24–30), the strategy does not change.

You'd think we should build a wall or hire security. At least we should pull up the weeds! But no, sowing the seed is the one and only strategy.

In Mark 4 we read a summary of everything these parables are teaching us:

> *This is what the kingdom of God is like. A man scatters seed on the ground. Night and day, whether he sleeps or gets up, the seed sprouts and grows, though he does not know how. All by itself the soil produces corn—first the stalk, then the ear, then the full grain in the ear. As soon as the corn is ripe, he puts the sickle to it, because the harvest has come.* **MARK 4:26–29**

The sower doesn't need to know how it all works. He doesn't even have to be awake—or present! He just needs to get the seed out there. From there on in, the seed does it all. And so these farming parables are all teaching one great truth: in the mission of the church, the Word is all powerful.

It might not *look* powerful. It probably looks weak and feels hit and miss. But there is life-giving, kingdom-growing, world-conquering power to the Word of God. The gospel we carry to the nations can be proclaimed simply—in 321!—but it is not simplistic. It is rich, profound and utterly fascinating. As you go into the world, full of obstacles and opposition, I want you to feel that you have a secret power. In your pocket you have seed, and if a single life-giving word falls on the right soil, dominions are brought down, life bursts forth, eternities are changed.

Yet all of that power lies in the seed, not in the sower. We just concern ourselves with the scattering, the rest is in God's hands. It's a lesson I've been learning for decades.

'YOU SOWED THE SEED'

Twenty years ago I was on staff at an incredibly evangelistic church. We worked hard midweek to reach the area and a very large proportion of those who came on Sunday were not Christians. Week by week we would offer Christ with warmth and welcome. And then there came my final sermon before leaving. I preached my heart out. I was in tears urging people to come to Jesus. At the end of the service I was in pieces, wondering what impact those words might have made—what impact *any* of my words had made over the years.

A friend of mine was on refreshments that Sunday. He approached me bearing a tray full of coffees and some of the most efficient pastoral care ever dispensed. He utterly changed my mood in four words. 'You sowed the seed,' he said, and then moved on with the tray. Instantly I was able to exhale, my shoulders dropped, my chest loosened. He was right. I had one job. I did that one job. I could move on.

The way we do mission is often filled with anxiety, fear, pride, pressure and guilt. We might claim to bear Jesus' word but we often fail to bear his demeanour. Jesus never had any anxiety about the prospects of his kingdom. He's the farmer with fistfuls of seed, chucking it with joyful abandon and making a glorious mess. Though birds peck, though sun scorches, though thorns choke, he knows: world domination beckons. The kingdom is coming, and it's coming through the low, slow, progress of the all-conquering seed.

So take heart. You have good seed. There is good soil. Sow.

321

FAQS

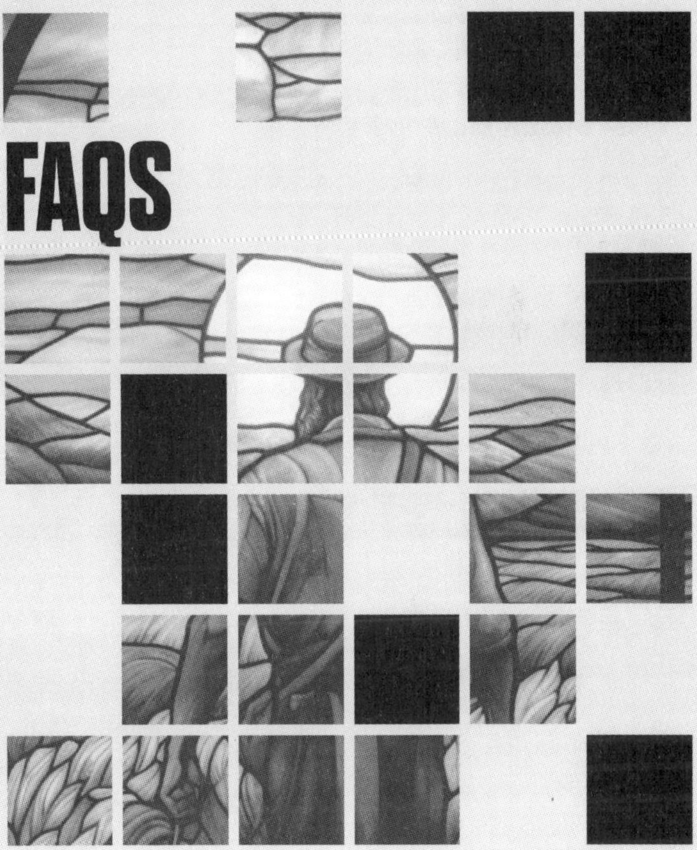

FAQS CONTENTS

321

WHY START WITH JESUS WHEN THE BIBLE DOESN'T?

Sometimes people object to the 321 outline because it begins with Jesus and with the THREE-ness of God. Should we begin this way if the Bible doesn't?

You could write books on this subject (and I have!). But let me answer briefly from John's Gospel.

The very first truth John shares with us is that God has *always* revealed himself in his Son. Jesus has been 'the Word' since 'the beginning' (John 1:1). Just a few verses later, John writes the same truth but from the other direction: 'No one has ever seen God; the only God, who is at the Father's side, he has made him known' (John 1:18, ESV). So it's doubly underlined in John's prologue: the Son of God is the one and only way to know God.

Saying this will provoke an urgent question: If that's true, how could God be known before Jesus?

But hopefully, looking at John 1, you can see the problem with the question. 'Before Jesus'? There *is* no before Jesus. Jesus, the Son of God, was there 'in the beginning'. He certainly wasn't human before his incarnation, but he was very active. In fact, everything the Father has ever done, he's done through his Son (John 5:17–23; Colossians 1:15–20; Hebrews 1:3).

Jesus is eternal. He has always been God's Word bringing light and life to the cosmos. So here's what the question is really asking: How was God known *before the incarnation—before Christmas?* To answer that question, John gives us the experience of three famous Old Testament believers: Moses, Abraham and Isaiah. All of them knew God, but how? John insists that they knew God by knowing Christ.

Moses wrote his Old Testament books as testimonies to *Jesus*. (Don't believe me? Check out John 5:36–47.) Abraham was excited to see *Jesus'* day, he saw it and was glad (read all about it in John 8:56–58). Isaiah saw *Jesus'* glory in the temple and wrote about *him* (see for yourself in John 12:36–41). Moses, Abraham and Isaiah were giants of the faith. But they were not Christ-less believers. There has never been such a thing as Christ-less faith. Because there has never been such a thing as a Christ-less God. As Jesus says, 'before Abraham was even born, I AM!' (John 8:58, NLT).

So the Jesus-God is the eternal God. The only God there has ever been is the God who is known through his Son.

The God who was 'in the beginning' is *not* an Almighty Loner. There has always been a Father making himself known through his Son, his Word, his radiant Light. If we haven't read the Old Testament in this way, John's Gospel will send us back to look again and see what was always there. As Jesus said, 'If you believed Moses, you would believe me, for he wrote about me' (John 5:46).

I've written some books to help: a Bible overview called *Long Story Short*, and an Old Testament devotional called *Reading Between the Lines Volume One* if you want to investigate more. But if you don't have time for those lengthier answers, I'll say it in short: 321 begins with Jesus because *everything* does!

IS IT REALLY NECESSARY TO DISCUSS THE TRINITY IN EVANGELISM?

Hopefully you've seen throughout this book and the 321 course that trinitarian evangelism is not about using complicated theological language. It's not about philosophical reflections on the nature of THREE-ness. It's not about imagining a 'heavenly group hug', perish the thought, or analogies of three-in-one-ness (like a shamrock or H2O). Almost every analogy brings more problems than it solves. Trinitarian evangelism is just about focusing our hearts and minds on the God who is revealed in his one and only Son.

Why make this explicit when we share our faith? Here are four reasons…

1. BECAUSE WE LOVE GOD

We speak about Father, Son and Spirit because that's who God is. And if evangelism is anything, it's talking about God! We don't want the most crucial truths about God to be sidelined or obscured. We want to see God for who he is and we want to let others in on the joy. We speak of Trinity because we love God, and...

2. BECAUSE WE LOVE JESUS

Imagine you have a gospel presentation that begins with a uni-personal God. Where will Jesus fit when he's introduced? He'll either sink down to the level of a prophet, a guru or an example. Or he'll be squished up into undifferentiated God-ness. He'll either be demoted or dissolved (for theology nerds, this is the choice between two heresies—Arianism or Modalism). The reason we're trinitarian is so we can speak rightly about Jesus. We need to be able to say that Jesus is both distinct from the Father and yet fully God. Only a trinitarian framework does justice to Christ's identity.

3. BECAUSE WE LOVE THE CROSS

Have you ever heard an illustration of the cross something like the following? (I have heard something like this quite often unfortunately.) There's a bus driver with 40 passengers. On one side of the road is a wall, on the other is a sheer drop into a canyon below. Suddenly, up ahead the driver sees his son, tied down, in the middle of the road.

The driver has a split second to decide: does he swerve off the cliff and kill the passengers; or stay on the road and kill his son? *Well the driver so loved his passengers that he ploughed over his helpless son... and*—so the illustration continues—*this is what God has done for us, killing Jesus instead of you. Won't you trust him?*

If non-Christians are repulsed by this vision—and many are—I don't blame them. Sometimes critics of the faith have called the cross 'cosmic child abuse'.

The problem with all such presentations is their failure to be trinitarian. That was the judgement of John Stott in his seminal work, *The Cross of Christ*:

> *...it is essential to affirm that the love, the holiness and the will of the Father are identical to the love, the holiness and the will of the Son. God was in Christ reconciling the world to himself.*[6]

Stott insists Christ is one with the Father in being—utterly unified in will—but he's not the same person as the Father. This is the heart of trinitarian theology: that there is one being of God and three persons. But the reason to press into this trinitarian language is not for its own sake. It's so that we can make sense of 'Christ and him crucified' (1 Corinthians 2:2).

---

6 John Stott, *The Cross of Christ* (IVP, 2006), p. 160.

Sometimes people say, *Don't complicate the gospel, just preach the cross*. I completely agree with the sentiment. But you can't preach the cross without a doctrine of the Trinity—or if you do, you'll preach an ugly caricature.

4. BECAUSE WE LOVE THE GOSPEL

If our gospel begins, 'There is an Almighty Loner…', how will such a story end? It might end up with God, the Almighty, empowering *us* to live our best lives. (Off we would run, trying to be powerful like God.) Or, it might end up with us flat on our faces before the Almighty. (Down we would bend, submitting *to* God.) But it won't end with adoption into the life of God forever. It won't end with us sharing the Father-Son love in the communion of the Spirit. It won't end with billions of children inheriting the cosmos as co-heirs *in* the Son. It won't end with: 'Bold I approach the eternal throne and claim the crown through Christ *my own*.'[7] It can't. If your gospel is not trinitarian, your good news cannot be that good.

---

7 Charles Wesley, 'And Can It Be' (1738).

WHAT DO WE ACTUALLY MEAN BY ORIGINAL SIN?

There are lots of definitions of original sin—some of them conflicting—so it's important to be clear. Here's what I mean by it: Everyone is equally and inescapably born into the same human family. That human family, like every family, already has a certain identity, character and destiny. I share in that identity, character and destiny by nature, not by choice.

Our *identity* begins with being made in God's image (Genesis 1:26) with all the dignity that entails, and at the same time, we're born 'in Adam' (1 Corinthians 15:22). That means we share in Adam's exile from God's presence. As those born east of Eden our natural state is disconnection from God, and the 'bad fruit' we bear is evidence of the 'bad tree' that we are in Adam (see Matthew 12:33). We sin because we are sinners. This means that our problem is much deeper than our behaviour, it's our being.

Our *character* is flawed from the outset. Just as I might be born predisposed to heart disease, I'm also born predisposed to suspicion, selfishness, slavery and all the other S's discussed in chapter 5. My sins might look different to yours in the particular ways they come out (just as my physical illnesses will look different to yours), but we all have a predisposition towards sin. Our characters share the family likeness of Adam.

Our *destiny* is death. Once again this has a physical and a spiritual dimension. The children of Adam inherit his flesh. We have a certain corruption which shows itself in our physical health and we have a certain corruption which shows itself in our moral behaviour. Because of our flesh, from the beginning, both physically and spiritually, our tendency is towards death. Apart from the intervention of God, the children of Adam perish—this destiny is a physical *and* a spiritual reality. Humans are born dying—born disconnected from God—and our natural end is judgement.

In one sense this is the most difficult truth we could possibly communicate to our friends and family. In another sense, it's the most grounded truth, completely earthed in something they already know. They know that they're born dying. Original sin upholds that truth and it refuses to proclaim some kind of fairytale escapism. Instead it takes our perishing state seriously. It simply insists that spiritual truths are profoundly connected to physical truths. In this way I consider original sin to be incredibly sane, grounded, honest, authentic and egalitarian. But, understandably, people still have objections. Hence the next FAQ…

IS THE ADAM STORY FAIR?

'Created sick and commanded to be well' is how anti-theist Christopher Hitchens put this objection.[8] It's a powerful line but it's a misunderstanding—a widespread one, unfortunately. Hitchens (representing so many others) thinks he's taking aim at the Adam and Christ story, but really he is critiquing something else: an Adam and Moses story.

An Adam and Moses story imagines that we are born in Adam, sharing in his sinful nature and estrangement. Now, though, we must follow Moses and his commandments back into God's presence. It would be the idea that we're born in exile but, by obeying the law, we can earn our way back.

You can imagine the equivalent when it comes to the Ann Forbes story. She's my ancestor discussed in chapter 5. Having committed theft, she was transported to Australia and now 6,000 of us have been 'born Australian'. My identity is down, in part, to one woman, one crime and

---

8 Christopher Hitchens, *Religion is a Force For Good—Christopher Hitchens*, online video recording, YouTube, 2 March 2014, <https://www.youtube.com/watch?v=VEMNpKkr2UI> [accessed 19 April 2024].

one exile. I didn't choose this Australian identity, instead my identity was determined long ago by events that were completely out of my hands.

This, in some ways, is like the Adam story. One man, through his own crime and punishment, has determined the identity of all his descendants. But when I compare this to the Ann Forbes story, there's a danger of misunderstanding. You might think the moral of the story is for Ann's Australian descendants to earn enough money to make it back to the mother country. That would certainly feel unfair. But that would be an Adam and Moses story—born estranged, earning our way back. The Adam and Christ version of the story is very different.

Imagine that Ann was not simply transported to Australia at His Majesty's pleasure. Imagine if King George III first exiled her and then promised to emigrate—declaring he would one day make his royal home in the Great Southern Land. He puts her in the place of judgement and he commits to joining her there. This is how the story runs in the Bible.

Adam and Eve were sent into exile, but their exile—our exile—becomes the very place where Christ meets us. We are born estranged, yet the King comes to meet us right where we are.

> *For God has bound everyone over to disobedience so that he may have* mercy *on them all.*
>
> **ROMANS 11:32, EMPHASIS MINE**

If original sin seems unfair (to us or to our friends) that's probably because it's *more* than fair, not less. The whole thing is set up on the foundation of mercy. It's not that we're 'created sick and commanded to be well'. It's more like: we're born sick and offered the Doctor; we're born hungry and offered Bread; we're born thirsty and offered Living Waters; we're born into a sinful condition and offered forgiveness. Mercy is what drives it all. Mercy is not fair, that's true. Mercy is better than fair.

We can explain to our friends that the God of original sin is not like the policeman waiting to see whether Ann Forbes will steal the cotton or not. The God of original sin is like the King who emigrates to Australia, joins his convicts and makes their prison a palace if only they'll receive him. If our friends can recognise that they, along with us all, *have* failed—if they see a spiritual sickness, hunger and thirst in themselves—the question becomes: which God can we trust? The Moral Policeman or the Emigrating King?

If our friend doesn't think they're a sinner, they certainly won't like being told they were born into it! But be patient with them. Explore how we're all living the Adam story. And pray they'll come to realise just how good the God of original sin is. He's the God who knows exactly what we're like—knows exactly where our stupidity takes us—and resolves to meet us there.

IS THE ADAM STORY TRUE?

Are we really asking our colleagues and neighbours to believe in epic tales of forbidden fruits, a garden paradise and a talking snake? This is a typically modern reaction to ancient stories. Around the world and down through history most people simply sit with such stories and appreciate their depths without instantly wanting to know whether it matches CCTV footage of the incident. In the modern West our reaction is 'pics or it didn't happen!'. But if we encounter that disposition in our friends (or in ourselves), it might be a good opportunity to talk about what the Bible is.

The Bible is a collection of 66 books from 40 different authors and encompasses many different genres: narratives; genealogies; poetry; instructions for ancient builders; instructions for ancient priests; instructions for ancient tribespeople; sayings; song lyrics; journal entries; letters; parables; dizzying visions; and more. It's like a disorienting but magnificent cathedral. The best way to appreciate a cathedral is not to study a thumbnail sketch of the floor plan and question its dimensions. To appreciate it, we go inside, we slow right down, and we try our best to experience it on its own terms. So it is with the Bible. We read poetry the way poetry's meant to be read. We read instructions to ancient peoples the way instructions to ancient peoples are meant to be read. We read parables the way parables are meant to be read. And when we come to the Adam story—well—how do we read that?

First we notice that Adam means humanity and so we get the idea: Humanity was on top of the world and then screwed it all up. That is a level of meaning that bears near infinite exploration. I've been reading the story for decades and continue to gain fresh insights from it. The truth of the story, on *that* level, is plain for anyone with an ounce of emotional intelligence. But having appreciated that, our friends still want to know (and rightly so), if it's true in a factual, historical sense. Did it happen?

My answer: Absolutely, though what CCTV would have captured I have no idea. The way back to the garden is barred in more ways than one. There are many senses in which we can't really enter paradise—I'd say our imagination is one. But yes, there was a historical figure called Adam, the father of the human race, whose fall entailed a fall for all. That's certainly the way the Apostle Paul took it:

> *For since death came through a man, the resurrection of the dead comes also through a man. For as in Adam all die, so in Christ all will be made alive.*
> **1 CORINTHIANS 15:21–22**

What does Paul assume? He assumes that Adam, just like Christ, is a historical figure whose actions have affected the world. So we have here a Scriptural non-negotiable: There's a representative called Adam whose actions determined the world for ill just as there's a representative called Christ whose actions determine the world for good. To put it succinctly: *Adam fell and Jesus rose*.

So, yes, Adam really is the father of the human race (see Acts 17:26) and his fall really has entangled us all. But talking to colleagues or friends about this, we don't have to take a 'stepping stones' approach. We don't have to establish agreement on Genesis 1 before moving to Genesis 2, and then establish agreement on Genesis 2 before moving to Genesis 3... If you ask me, that's not the way the Bible, or Christianity, or evangelism works. Our way in is always Jesus. As it is with God, and with creation, so it is with Adam—Jesus is our starting point.

Therefore we can say to our friend: 'I'm not sure what I would do to prove the historicity of Genesis chapter 3 but the New Testament puts it like this: *Adam fell and Jesus rose*. Why don't we consider the second half of that? Because if Jesus rose, then he is who the Bible says he is—the Second Adam—and he vindicates the story.'

I don't think you first establish the literalness of Adam's fall and then turn to Christ's resurrection. I think you can do it the other way around. Beginning with Jesus really is the answer—to everything!

For further study, from shortest to longest, you can read:

- My FAQ in *How to See Life: A Guide in 321*;
- *Is Easter Unbelievable?* by Rebecca McLaughlin;
- *The Case for the Resurrection of Jesus* by Gary R. Habermas and Michael R. Licona.

IS EVERY CHRISTIAN AN EVANGELIST?

Every Christian is part of a missionary body called the church. We are all priestly. Think of how Peter puts it as he addresses a bedraggled mob of refugees in northern Turkey, clinging on to Christ by their fingernails:

> *But you are a chosen people, a royal priesthood, a holy nation, God's special possession, that you may declare the praises of him who called you out of darkness into his wonderful light.* **1 PETER 2:9**

To the surrounding culture they looked like they were bottom of the heap. To God they are chosen, royal and priestly! What does it mean to be priestly? Think of the Levites of the Old Testament. They were a group within Israel who acted as go-betweens. They stood between God and the people, bringing the two together. And here Peter says that the church plays that go-between role. We bring God to the world and the world to God. But notice that we do it *together.* The 'you' of this verse is plural. We are not a club of individual evangelists. We are a community of love, and that community is priestly.

Sometimes people talk about 'the priesthood of all believers' which is a precious truth when properly understood. It's the idea that each member of the body of Christ belongs to this royal priesthood, not just the clergy or the monks and nuns. In this sense, no one is more priestly than anyone else. We are all equally a part of this giant witness called the church which is sent into the world.

Unfortunately we have individualised so many things in the West and this is one more example: we have made evangelism into a task for individuals—a task which each individual must equally fulfil. But in the Bible, the church as a whole is God's go-between. It's not 'the priesthood of each individual believer', it's 'the priesthood of *all believers'*—going as ONE.

There are many implications of this truth, but one is this: not everyone within the priesthood will have the same gifting, calling or opportunities. We're all different. Some will be capital-E Evangelists, specifically gifted by the Spirit and tasked by the church in the role of proclaiming good news (see Ephesians 4:11). Some will do the *work* of an evangelist (2 Timothy 4:5). And many, many more Christians—the whole church—will be witnesses, through life and lip, to the grace of Jesus (Acts 1:8). In setting out these different roles, the New Testament is not at all afraid to say that different Christians are differently gifted in the missionary task.

We know this is true with other gifts. Some people are capital-P Pastors—they have that role and that gifting. Some people don't have the formal job title but they are gifted by God to be incredibly pastoral. But all Christians are called to play a role in the flock as we're shepherded by Jesus. It's the same with evangelism. We all play a role but it's not always the same role.

Later in Peter's first letter he gives the shortest 'gifts list' in the New Testament. In fact he only mentions two: speakers and servers (1 Peter 4:10–11). Some Christians have the gift of the gab, and some don't. If you don't have the gift, that doesn't mean you keep silent at all times. You should still 'be prepared' with words of witness as Peter's previous chapter instructs (1 Peter 3:15). But there is such a thing as gifting and it's OK to acknowledge that, just as we do with pastoral giftings.

By the same token, some Christians have a real gift when it comes to hospitality. I don't have this gift. My culinary skills extend to a microwave and the 'defrost' setting. But others—my goodness—they have such a gift for opening up their homes and welcoming people in. That doesn't mean I'm off the hook when it comes to serving. I'm still called to serve and there are still times when servers are called to speak. But we're not all wired the same, and these differences are good and God-given.

What's more, when you weave together these distinctives, you get a wonderful vision for evangelism. Imagine homes and tables opened up to the world. And then imagine Christians liberally sprinkled around the dinner tables who are particularly good with words. You've just imagined one of Jesus' favourite evangelistic strategies (e.g. Luke 5:27–32), and the way mission unfolded in Acts, and in the early church.

The church is *not* a refuelling station for a bunch of Lone Ranger evangelists. And not every Christian is gifted in the same way. But we are *all* gifted so that we fit together within this missionary body called church. So think of the gifts you have. Think of the gifts of those closest to you in the church. Are there ways you could collaborate to bring hospitality and speaking gifts together in outreach? Perhaps you could run a 321 course with a meal each session—a wonderful integration of word and welcome. That's just one suggestion, you can think of many more. May the Spirit give wisdom and inspiration.

WHAT DO I SAY IF I'M GIVEN 90 SECONDS?

It doesn't happen *very* often but just yesterday somebody told me that her boss once called her into his office and said, 'Right, you have 60 seconds. Convince me of Christianity.' She took about a minute and a half to do it and he still reminds her of those 90 seconds years later.

I've also had quite a few opportunities to say to people in the middle of a faith conversation: 'Look, we're a bit lost in the weeds. Can I go to 30,000 feet and give you a bird's eye view of Christianity?' Getting that perspective can really help. So often you'll find that friends and family are discussing something (or *despising* something) that's not at all what Christians are saying. So it's worth taking a moment to get the big picture. And if your friend is at all interested, they should be fine with you taking 90 seconds to tell the Christian story. But then the question becomes: What do you say?

Well we've got our Speak Life YouTube channel where dozens of videos offer a quick Christianity 101. We've also got the 321 course, so do make use of 321course.com. But below I've written out 286 words that I used one day when a friend challenged me to summarise Christianity. I was being interviewed and the cameras were rolling. So once I'd done it they turned it into a video and many people have since been helped. Let me share the words I used at the time because they're not super polished and you're very welcome to steal, adapt and improve:

In the beginning there was light and life and love: a Father loving his Son, Jesus, in the joy of the Holy Spirit. And everything has come from light and life and love. But we look today at the world and we see it's not like that. We see a world full of darkness and death and disconnection. Where's that come from?

Well, we've turned from the light, and when you turn from light, where else do you go but darkness? When you turn from love, where else do you go but disconnection? When you turn from life, where else do you go but death? But then what does love do, when love sees the beloved in trouble?

Love says: 'Your pit will be my pit, your debts will be my debts, your darkness will be my darkness, your death will be my death.'

So who is Jesus? He's the Son of the Father who came as our Brother, to be *with us* in the darkness, to take that darkness on himself—that death, that disconnection that we all deserve for turning from God—he took it on himself on the cross, plunging it down to the hell that it deserves. And he rose up again to light and life and love. And he says: 'You in the darkness, do you want my light? You in death, do you want my life? You in disconnection, do you want my love?'

And anyone who turns and says Yes to Jesus, we now belong to him. We get his Father as our Father, we get his Spirit as our Spirit, we get his future as our future. It's for free and it's forever. So do you want Jesus?

321

WHAT NOW?

Well done for completing *How to Speak Life.* Hopefully now you have a number of resources to help you in your personal evangelism.

You've thought about life according to Jesus and appreciated again God's THREE-ness, the world's TWO-ness and your ONE-ness.

You've seen afresh the outgoing, life-giving goodness of God and have been inspired to join him in his missionary purposes.

You've been prayerfully considering friends and family who need to hear this good news and you've been reflecting on how best to reach them.

You have been thinking through the eight seeds that you can scatter in personal conversations. You've thought about how you'd speak them out in ways that are natural to you and will connect with your friends.

Perhaps too you have been challenged to consider changes you can make in your life and witness. As we finish, it's worth reflecting on these.

SPEND SOME TIME CONSIDERING YOUR OWN ANSWERS. YOU MAY WANT TO JOT DOWN SOME THOUGHTS HERE...

Has your thinking about evangelism changed as you've read through *How to Speak Life*? If so, how?

Which of the 'seeds' do you think might be most helpful in your personal witness?

Have you had the chance to sow any of them recently? How did it go?

____

____

____

____

Are there changes you feel challenged to make? Perhaps think of…

- Praying for open doors, mouths and hearts
- Rejecting 'Up and In' evangelism
- Pursuing 'Down and Out' opportunities
- Resolving to 'let your light shine' and not to hide it
- Identifying your particular gifts and using them
- Collaborating with others in outreach
- What has most encouraged you as you've read the book?

MOVING FORWARDS

Let me suggest three very practical things you can do from here that will apply the lessons of *How to Speak Life*.

If you haven't already done the 321 course, why not do it now. You can watch the whole thing in a couple of hours, or let it sink in over eight sessions. Nothing inspires evangelism better than being evangelised, so hear the good news again.

Share the course with others. It's been designed so that you can evangelise your friends with the flick of a text message. 'Hey, I've just been watching this introduction to Jesus. I think you'd really like it. Why not check out episode one and you can tell me what you think when we meet up… 321course.com.'

Even better, put on the course in person. It's free and everything you need to run the course is on the website. If possible, involve a meal and as much time for discussion as you can. But the course is designed to be flexible, so run it the way that makes sense in your context.

And if Speak Life can serve you in your evangelism, let us know. We have over 1,000 videos on our YouTube channel and 500 podcasts (and counting!) all aimed at helping you to love Jesus and share Jesus. Find out more at speaklife.org.uk.